D0772389

1/8

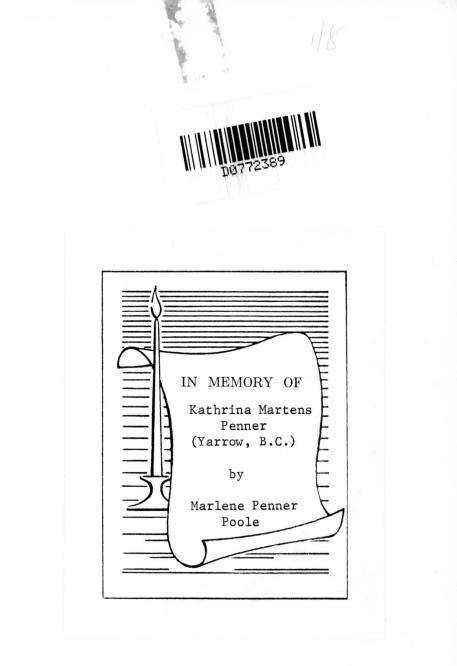

IN MEMORY OF

Kathrina Martens
Penner
(Yarrow, B.C.)

by

Marlene Penner
Poole

IS 'HOLY SCRIPTURE' CHRISTIAN?

BS
2395
E9

CHRISTOPHER *Francis* EVANS

Is 'Holy Scripture' Christian?

and other questions

*

WITHDRAWN

SCM PRESS LTD

13256

HIEBERT LIBRARY
PACIFIC COLLEGE · M. B. SEMINARY
FRESNO, CALIF. 93702

Chapter 1, 'Tradition and Scripture', first appeared in
Religious Studies 3, 1967, pp. 323-37
from which it is reprinted
by kind permission of the Editor

334 00723 2

First published 1971
by SCM Press Ltd
56 Bloomsbury Street, London

© SCM Press Ltd 1971

Printed in Great Britain by
Northumberland Press Limited
Gateshead

Contents

	Preface	vii
1	Tradition and Scripture	1
2	Is 'Holy Scripture' Christian?	21
3	Should the New Testament be taught to Children?	37
4	Is 'the Jesus of History' Important?	51
5	Resurrection in the New Testament and Now	64
6	Is the New Testament Church a Model?	78
7	Commitment	91
	Index of Subjects	109
	Index of Names	111

Preface

These lectures were mostly delivered in the first instance in Canberra under the auspices of the Council and Warden of St Mark's Library and Institute of Theology, to whom I can convey only very inadequate thanks both for their initial invitation to spend a sabbatical leave as their guest and also for the kindness which they lavished on me. The lectures are somewhat random, since most – though not quite all – of their subjects were not of my own choosing but at the request of others, as is also their publication. They represent presumably the kind of subjects which an interested audience wished to hear about, and of which they expected their visitor to be able to give some kind of report. If for no other reason, they do not aim at, nor achieve, any unity of theme or presentation. In this respect they may perhaps reflect one feature of theological, or at any rate New Testament studies, at the present time, which is their incompleteness and consequent inconclusiveness.

· This is a feature which perhaps has never been, and ought not to be, wholly absent from theology. The New Testament is a singular noun referring to a single something; but that its contents, which were written for a variety of purposes and to a variety of conditions, constitute a coherent unity is not immediately obvious and plain for all to see. It has generally been a matter of faith and doctrine. Already within the New Testament itself there is evidence that early Christian thinkers felt the need of placing the gospel message and the gospel events within the context of the Old Testament in order to make fuller sense of them. Theologians of subsequent centuries were impelled to place them in the theological and philosophical contexts of their own times so that they might be seen to answer the questions of their own times. Only rarely, and seldom for very long, has the New Testament been held both to be a self-evident unity and also itself to supply the wherewithal for interpreting itself as a whole. The critical and historical analysis with which biblical study has had to learn to live in the last century and a half, in paying particular attention to the conditions in which revealed truth has been given, has tended to underline this feature of incompleteness. In this it has pressed very hard upon the religious mind with its disposition towards unities which received classic expression in the words of the Epistle to the Ephesians, 'one body and one Spirit, even as also you were called in one hope of your calling; one Lord, one faith, one baptism, one God and Father of all' – though in this the religious mind is probably only voicing what is a disposition of the human mind as such.

This pressure of critical analysis may appear at almost any point. Thus, in relation to the New Testament as a whole Dr Kurt Aland, in his lecture *The Problem of the New Testament Canon*, first traces the principles or lack of them which went to the making of the New Testament canon and then reaches the present situation, which is that not only individuals but also churches in fact operate with a canon within the canon. This he pronounces intolerable. But why is it intolerable, unless the past is held to be completely prescriptive in this matter for the present? May not the fact that this has been the situation for so long argue that it has to be tolerated and lived with? If not, are we to wait for the solution which Aland propounds of arriving at a canon which is agreed between the churches and is actual, or must we press on as best we may, leaving this unsolved problem in our rear? It is intolerable in Aland's view because 'the variety in the actual Canon in its different forms is not only the standard symptom, but simultaneously also the real cause of its [Christianity's] illness. This illness – which is in blatant conflict with the unity which is fundamental to its nature – cannot be tolerated'.[1] But even if this is the case – and the unity in faith of the churches of the first two centuries did not depend on the possession and use of an agreed canon – it only pushes the pressure further back. For what in essence is the church? This question is likely to be the starting-point of any venture in that ecumenical movement which is so clearly the task of our own time. But when the New Testament is analysed critically, that is, when its separate voices are allowed to speak with their historical distinctness and individuality and not simply in so far as they can be made to speak with one voice, is it so evident that its documents are designed to supply the answer to this question, or at any rate an answer sufficiently solid and detailed to serve the purposes of the reunion of Christendom? Whether it is legitimate to speak of 'the church' at all in the New Testament except as a kind of shorthand, and how far particular formulations of belief and spiritual life are contingent or have a more lasting validity as norms, may turn out to be a series of problems whose solution we cannot wait upon before getting on with what needs to be done. And behind the church, by any Christian confession, stands the Lord Jesus. But how far and in what way does he stand behind the church? This is a vexed question of 'the historical Jesus'. The fact that this question can be asked at all, and that the analysis of the New Testament documents has led to it as a legitimate question, may turn out to be of more lasting significance than any answers which scholars or groups of scholars may come up with, at least so long as the historical element is held to be vital to Christianity. For once on the basis of analysis of the documents a distinction has been made between words and actions of a historical Jesus which made way for varied consequences, and words and actions ascribed to him which had grown out of those varied consequences, the historical core of the gospel takes on permanently the character of a sliding scale of cause and effect with no great prospect that it can be fixed at a point agreeable to all.

In this way the modern theologian, and not only in the biblical fields, is denied the methodical approach of his predecessors, who from a number of assured results were able to erect systems with one firm stone superimposed upon another. He has to learn to live with incompleteness and inconclusiveness at almost every point, and to forge ahead regardless. This is not, however, a situation which is wholly negative. On the contrary, it has certain features of a positive kind not unrelated to the character of his material. After all, his subject matter is in the end God himself, and God may not be captured in a system nor even be held to be the ground of a system, however clearly he may have spoken or acted. It is not simply obscurantism to be reminded that *omnia abeunt in mysterium*. Already within the New Testament itself there is, at least to the modern exegete, something of a tension between the indirect, oblique and largely parabolic character of the words and actions of Jesus which is still visible in the synoptic gospels, and the more fixed and dogmatic terminology of the epistles and of subsequent theology, even when that terminology is still largely the language of images. This parabolic character of Christian truth, and therefore of human life, is not ensured simply, or even at all, by repeating the parables of Jesus. As appears in the Fourth Gospel, which has no such parables but places all under the 'sign', it appertains to the whole, even when in Christ the sign is identified with what it signifies. It is more likely to be appreciated by the expositor, using that word in its widest sense, or by the theologian when he turns expositor, and it is at the heart of that branch of theological study which has assumed central importance at the present time, viz. 'hermeneutics', which is the study of meaning at all the levels at which it emerges.

NOTE

1. K. Aland, *The Problem of the New Testament Canon*, Mowbray, 1962, p.31.

I

Tradition and Scripture

Tradition in either of its two senses – the act of handing on (generally verbally), and what is handed on – is a particular instance of a law of human existence that men live in dependence on one another and by the processes of giving and receiving. So a sociologist can write, 'If we are to be able to speak of real tradition, we must find the past spontaneously taken into account as the meaning of the present, without any discontinuity in social time, and without any consideration of the past as irrelevant'.[1] 'If democracy,' wrote Chesterton, 'means that I give a man a vote even though he is my chauffeur, tradition means that I give a man a vote even though he is my great-great-grandfather.' What is handed on, however, is not existence of a purely biological kind, to remain always what it has been or to change very slowly over a space of aeons. Except in primitive tribes even tradition is not simply passed on as something static and timeless, and it is received by men who, though themselves in time, are not wholly time-bound or restricted by what they receive. They believe themselves to be capable of significant action which is more than the repetition and reproduction of what has gone before. They are able to grasp a span of time and to call it history; they believe themselves to have a history, and they write history.

Both concepts, those of tradition and of history, have to do with the relation of the past to the present, with the way in which the past becomes present, and therefore inevitably with the authority under which men live. Since these are among the few really great issues of human existence, it is not surprising that they have aroused bitter controversy. This is illustrated in our time by the fact that the bitterest *odium theologicum* is to be found among, and in reaction to, existentialists, who are busier than most have been in denying any relevance to the past, and in asserting that men live under no authority but their own in an existence which has to be made up as one goes along. That the Christian church has so often been, and still is, involved in controversy on this matter is simply testimony to the truth that Christianity does not live apart from human existence or as an addition to it, but as a recapitulation and intensification of it, a focussing and clarification of it. What men live by in order to be human receives in the Christian faith a concentrated form. The church also lives by tradition and history; it has a very special concern with the relation between the past and the present, with how the past is to become the present, and with the question of the authority under which men live. And since in this case the past is a past which is specially associated with a unique relationship set up between men and God, and the authority under which men are to live is the authority of God, it is not surprising that there has been bitter controversy over this matter in the church.

But while the Christian faith recapitulates, intensifies and focusses human existence, it has its own distinctive way of doing so, and its own special version of this matter has been governed by its character and origins. This takes the form of some conjunction of tradition and scripture – either tradition and scripture, or scripture and tradition, or tradition – scripture, or scripture – tradition, or tradition (scripture) or scripture (tradition). All these positions, and others which can hardly be represented by a simple conjunction between the two terms, have been held in some parts of the church at some time or other. The gospel produced a faith in God and a way of life in community expressive of that faith. So far it followed a common pattern, and was hardly at all peculiar. But Christianity is unique among the great religions in being born with a Bible in its cradle. This was entirely peculiar. The Old Testament as sacred scripture was unique in the civilized world at the time. Neither the Greeks nor the Romans had anything really like it. Its influence upon the first Christians, upon their faith and their life in community, was incalculable. It can be seen or traced in manifold forms – in the frequent use by New Testament writers of the formula 'Scripture says' (as the NEB rightly renders it), in the straightforward citation of the Old Testament to prove or bolster a point, in its use to present the gospel in terms of 'fulfilment', or in the evoking of a whole theology by a phrase or word. It can even be that the Old Testament was held to furnish facts and information about the gospel itself – if scripture said 'Out of Egypt have I called my son' then the Christ must have gone to Egypt and been brought back thence. But the influence goes deeper, and has been operating at a formative level before Christians put pen to paper. The aim of a book such as C. H. Dodd's *According to the Scriptures*[2] is to seek to penetrate to 'the substructure of New Testament theology', and to peer through the windows of the early Christian workshop, since in the earliest days the Old Testament supplied the Christians with their first, perhaps their only, theological categories. Hence one early Christian position is likely to have been scripture *and* tradition, or scripture (tradition), where scripture is the Old Testament, and tradition is such verbal statements of faith as were deemed necessary to make a Christian. How many of such statements one had to know and believe at any one time or place we do not know. Was it sufficient in Pauline churches simply to receive the statements which Paul, using the technical terminology of oral tradition, rehearses as the original gospel he had preached – that Christ died for our sins, was buried, was raised the third day and appeared (I Cor. 15.3)? How much or how little did one have to know through oral transmission about Jesus in order to be a Christian in Antioch, Corinth, Ephesus or Rome in AD 40, 50, 60, or 70? We have no means of answering these questions. But perhaps the position at some times and in some places would have been better denoted by scripture-tradition, since it would seem that part at least of oral tradition (perhaps a great part) consisted of Christian exegesis of the Old Testament in the light of central gospel truths.

But here already there is a complication, which is reflected in the ambivalent attitude in New Testament writings towards both tradition and scripture. 'Tradition' is in the New Testament both a good and a bad word. On the one hand Paul, as already observed, can for all his freedom use the technical language of tradition, 'I handed on what I received', in rehearsing the basic facts of the gospel, as he can do also with reference to the eucharist in I Cor. 11, although here he complicates the matter by saying that what he handed on was what he had received (by tradition) from the Lord (whatever that may mean). He can exhort the Corinthians to hold fast the 'traditions' which he had handed on to them (I Cor. 11.2), and the Thessalonians to hold to the 'traditions' which they had been taught by him either by word or letter (II Thess. 2.15), and to walk 'according to the paradosis which you received from me' (3.6). We have no means of knowing what any of these traditions was, nor whether they entered permanently into the faith and life of the churches or church. Later and more 'traditional' voices can refer to the 'holy commandment traditioned' to Christians (II Peter 2.21), and to the faith once for all 'traditioned' to the saints (Jude 3). On the other hand, Paul warns against a paradosis of men (Col. 2.8), and the only reference to tradition in the gospels, as distinct from the tradition or act of passing on which was responsible for the gospels, is the hostile one to 'the tradition of the elders' (Mark 7.3-13), which seems to mean the oral judgments of Jewish theologians glossing the written text and making it applicable. The ground of hostility is that this tradition obscures and weakens the force of central tenets in the Law. But there is also an ambivalent attitude to scripture. For all that the Old Testament had such influence in forming early Christian theology it did not go uncriticized, by implication if not explicitly. Here again the evidence is obscure. How are we to evaluate a saying like 'Not one jot or tittle of the law shall fall until all things are fulfilled' when it stands alongside in the same gospel 'They of old time (meaning scripture) said, but I say unto you'? Do both come from the same lips, or is the first a product of a Jewish Christianity in conflict with Judaism? There was, however, sufficient radical statement in the gospels to undermine eventually the authority of the Old Testament as some had conceived that authority; while Paul's critique of the Law, and the rather different critique in the Epistle to the Hebrews of the Law as a shadow and as destined to pass away as the old before the new, were bound to lead to an alteration of the status of scripture (the Old Testament) in face of something else which was not yet written. When we pass from these earlier days to the end of the first century and on into the second we pass, as is well known, into a period of obscurity, in which there are only a few shafts of light from such Christian writings as have survived from the period, and the shafts do not always fall on what we would most like to see and know. We shall be looking for answers to such questions as, 'How does this or that writer regard scripture (the Old Testament)?' 'Does he show evidence of knowing

Christian writings alongside scripture?' 'How does he regard them?' 'How has he come by the Christianity he professes?' 'Of what kind is this Christianity?' These questions are difficult to answer. It does not follow, for example, that because a writer does not mention a New Testament writing he did not know it; but we cannot say that he did know it unless he mentions or clearly quotes it. If he appeals to it, it does not follow that he is treating it as scripture, since there are at least three stages on the way to canonization. A book may be appealed to simply as a good book, its authority lying in its spiritual quality; it may be appealed to because it is believed to have been written by one who is his own authority, for example, an apostle; it may be appealed to simply because it is in the canon, that is, in the books permitted to be read, and that is its authority.

As an illustration of the different positions which could be held we may cite I Clement and Ignatius' epistles. For Clement scripture is the Old Testament. His letter is to a considerable extent made up of quotation from it, and he can settle the main questions, including the ministry with which he is principally concerned, by reference to it. He knows I Corinthians (and only one letter to the Corinthians), from which he derives examples and encouragement, since it was concerned with a similar subject of strife in the church. He knows sayings of Jesus, almost certainly in oral form, but refers to them for support only after his appeal to the Old Testament. His language reflects the Epistle to the Hebrews, but in a way which may indicate that this has become part of the liturgy at Rome, and in arguing for ministerial order he refers to tradition in the form that the Lord appointed apostles, who themselves appointed their successors, who appointed bishops (if that is the right interpretation of a difficult passage). Here we seem to have a position which might be summed up as scripture and tradition, or scripture-tradition. By contrast Ignatius shows so little evidence of the use of the Old Testament that it has been seriously maintained by scholars (e.g. W. L. Knox[3]) that he did not know it except through a book of *Testimonia*, though how one could be a bishop of Antioch without knowing it is difficult to conceive. In Philad. 8.2 he refers to a dispute on the matter:

When I heard some people saying, 'If I do not find it in the archives I do not believe it' [scripture-tradition?], I answered them

'But it is written there.' They retorted, 'That is just the question.' To my mind it is Jesus Christ who is the original documents; the inviolable archives are his cross and death and resurrection, and the faith that came by him.

The impatience with which he breaks off the discussion shows where his heart lay, and while Ignatius certainly knows several Pauline epistles and uses them to effect, and probably knows St Matthew's Gospel though making little use of it, he is primarily a witness to a church life of considerable richness, whose inner meaning he interprets christologically and by reference to traditional kerygmatic statements which are one of the principal features of his letters. Ignatius is thus evidence for the position tradition (scripture). When we pass to Justin in the middle of the second century the position is again different. He is a witness that in worship 'the memoirs of the apostles' (whatever precisely that may mean, and scholars are seldom quite sure that they know what it means) are read alongside the prophets (the Old Testament?), and there are quotations from the memoirs to settle points, but Paul's name is not mentioned and the alleged quotations from him are dubious. As Harnack wrote,

> No one that reads Justin's Dialogue with Trypho but can receive the liveliest impression that the author is simply crying for a New Testament; but, seeing that he cannot produce it *directly as a fundamental document* he is compelled to write endless chapters and laboriously to construct it for himself from the Old Testament and the history of Jesus (the Gospels)! If he could have quoted as the Word of God in the strict sense *one only* of the dozens of appropriate passages in St Paul, and could have been able to refer to the *books of the New Covenant* – how much simpler and shorter his whole task would have been.[4]

Justin is a witness, perhaps, for tradition-scripture. How powerful this position was for a long time appears from the remark of Papias, who already knew at least two written gospels, that he lost no opportunity of interrogating the elders and their disciples, since he thought books less profitable than a voice which lives and abides. From this particular position, while not necessarily agreeing with the dictum of Widengren that the reduction to writing of an oral tradition is always a sign of a loss of nerve, or with a reported saying of R. H. Lightfoot that the writing of the gospels was an early manifestation of the operation of original sin in the church, we might have to reverse the well-known statement of Dr C. K. Barrett, and say that scripture represents the worldliness of the church and tradition points to its supernatural origin and basis, since the gospel is communicated from person to person by word of mouth, and even when written is only able to become the Word of God when turned back again into oral address, which process it often resists just by being written.

However, matters did not stop there. In a comparatively short period of time, and by processes no longer traceable (some think it was Marcion who hit on the idea), a New Testament canon is formed. This is not the place to enter into the details of this complex question; suffice it to say that about the turn of the second century there is, in such important Christian centres as we have knowledge of, a canonical New Testament, though not necessarily the same in each place. The Catholic epistles, apart from I Peter and I John, are not admitted into the Syrian church until the fourth (fifth?) century; Hebrews is not yet admitted in the West, and there are doubts about Revelation. But in principle the die is cast, and further developments will lie along the line of increasing unanimity in the churches as to what the New Testament is. This creates a new situation. It is now impossible to talk of scripture and tradition, or *vice versa*, in the old sense, since what had previously been tradition has now itself become scripture, modelled on and assimilated to what had previously been known as authoritative scripture, only more so, for as a 'new covenant' in a two-volume bible it was bound by its very designation as 'new' to demote what has now to be labelled 'old'. The authority under which Christians were to live had now become increasingly a bookish authority.

This new development, which was to shape the pattern of Christian life and authority from that time onwards, had a number of consequences.

(i) It was responsible for introducing a tendency to fudge the evidence. This was due to the curious nature of the new canon, and the necessity which was felt to justify its existence and character. Thus it contained – no one knew (or knows) how – four gospels, despite the fact that 'gospel' in Christian usage was by definition a singular noun. Everyone knows the knots into which Irenaeus tied himself in adducing reasons, natural and mystical, why there had to be four gospels, and the Muratorian Canon justified the Fourth Gospel (and perhaps argued its pre-eminence) by the 'cock and bull story'[5] of John's writing it in the name of the rest of the apostles after a three-day fast. The canon also contained Pauline letters, which had been occasional documents directed to specific and limited situations, and in which could be found not only his great statements on justification and on the church as Christ's body, but also his remarks on women's hair and on Timothy's dyspepsia. How was this to be justified as holy scripture? The author of the Muratorian Canon, whom some think to have been Hippolytus, and if so an influential voice in Rome at the turn of the second century, is not at a loss. Paul, he says, restricted his writing to churches seven in number in imitation of the author of Revelation, and since seven is a sacred number of completeness he was really all the time addressing the whole church. It is true that the Pastorals do not fit into this scheme, but they are dragged into it on the ground that, though written to individuals, they are really concerned with the church's discipline. Since the Muratorian Canon is uncertain where the line should be drawn at the end of the canon no rationale is given for the Catholic Epistles (though later on the same appeal to the number seven was to be made), but Acts, as the odd man out, has to be justified, and is so on the ground that it is the Acts of all the apostles as opposed to the Acts of a single apostle, which Haenchen dubs 'an optical illusion'. But more widespread, even universal, was the necessity felt to justify all New Testament books as 'apostolic' in the literal sense of that word, and this is done by means of arguments and traditions which in the eyes of the modern scholar are highly suspect if not valueless.

(ii) A second consequence was to bind the New Testament and the Old together. This made permanent a position which had obtained in earlier times, for example, in I Clement, where scripture is the Old Testament, and it put an end, perhaps in reaction against Marcion, to questions which had been asked about the Old Testament. More than one position had been canvassed; for example, in the Letter of Ptolemy to Flora discrimination is made between different parts of the Pentateuch, upon which the comment has been made that if his threefold division of the law had been accepted by the early church the problems of modern criticism might have been much less pressing.

But this question was now foreclosed, and the only way out was allegorical exegesis. This had already appeared in the Epistle of Barnabas, was further developed by the Alexandrian Fathers, entered the blood-stream of the West through Ambrose's acquaintance with eastern theology, and was our heritage until yesterday (again not without a considerable element of fudging), until we were released from it by what some think an equally dubious device, the doctrine of progressive revelation.

(iii) A third consequence was that the problem of scripture and tradition did not disappear when tradition became scripture; it stayed on, but in a different form. It did so because what had become scripture was only in part what had been tradition (the Pauline epistles contained tradition, but had not themselves been tradition), and because part of what had been tradition had not become scripture. By the time the canon was formed the church (or, the churches) had produced a life and a style. Men became Christians in response to preaching, or, as now, by attraction to the community and by discovery of what went on in it. They were baptized into a faith which was increasingly formulated, and were instructed by a catechism which was developing. They participated in a liturgy communicating divine realities which had received, and were still receiving, expression. They adopted a way of life. What was the basis and authority of all this, and what was its relation to the newly formulated canon? There is no single answer to such questions; there might be different answers in each case, and our picture will depend on whose writings have survived. Thus R. P. C. Hanson, in his book *Origen's Doctrine of Tradition*, draws a distinction between two writers who have left a good deal of material on which to form a judgment. Clement of Alexandria appears to have believed in a secret unwritten tradition of doctrine, and did so as a real Gnostic for whom there was a spiritual aristocracy and *élite* in the church to whom this tradition was fitted. Origen also believed in a secret tradition, but it was connected more closely with common Christian institutions, and as a biblicist he made little use of it.[6] In other authors it was a question of the relation between scripture and the *regula fidei* or the creed:

While Irenaeus regarded Scripture as the rule of faith side by side with the rule of Christian doctrine, the Creed being a sort of digest of the most indispensable articles of Scripture, Tertullian goes further and ranks the Creed above Scripture. He was forced to this by controversy with heretics, cf. *De Praesc.* 17-20, where he complains that appeal to Scripture will never convince heretics. Heretics have their own canon of Scripture.[7]

Plainly each of the early Fathers would have to be interrogated in turn, but there is one general observation which has been made about the Fathers which, if correct, has considerable bearing on the matter. Père Bouyer[8] has written in the following sense: To attempt to arrive at a one-sided answer to the question of scripture and tradition is doomed to failure, since the Fathers can quite cheerfully say at one moment that the whole of the faith is contained in the scriptures, and at another with equal confidence that scripture is of no avail without tradition as its complement or supplement, and they are able to speak like this because they do not think, as we have tended to do whether Catholic or Protestant, of the faith as a list of propositions in divinity, but as a unity, a single living object under multiple forms. Moreover they do not mean by scripture primarily an authority under which we live, but a whole world in which we live, and everything in the world to be read through it, and the whole world to be found in it. This wholeness, without which neither the letter nor the spirit of scripture can be grasped, is proliferated in the living gospel of the church, which, while always consonant with scripture, is not dependent on it, and its purpose is to prevent us from maiming the data of scripture through a minimizing or distorting interpretation.

If this is a judicious summary of the thought of the Fathers as a whole (in so far as they can be taken as a whole), it may be important, for it indicates that the main drive of a doctrine of tradition lies in the sense of living in, and out of, a Christian wholeness of life, and those institutions, customs, ways of going on which communicated and ministered this were loved and valued, even if the form which this love took was to ascribe to them the same bogus apostolic origin as had been given to the canonical books.

In this way the patristic doctrine of tradition came to take the form of a doctrine of unwritten apostolic traditions, and it appears in this guise at the Council of Trent as part of a double theory of Christian truth. The chief difficulty about this doctrine has been to discover what it is. Catholic writers on the matter appear to be fugitive about it. Thus the author of the article 'Tradition' in the *Catholic Encyclopaedia*, after making the usual debating points that the church made the canon and that scripture does not interpret itself – which in themselves are quite good points – discourses for several pages on traditions without giving instances, except that we would not know that Sunday was the Christian day of worship without information from the Lord via the apostles, which is hardly a convincing example, as one could easily think of other reasons. Considering that in the Reformation controversy the existence of unwritten traditions going back to the Lord or the apostles was almost as much an *articulus aut stantis aut cadentis ecclesiae* on the Catholic side as were *sola fide* or *sola scriptura* on the other side, one would have expected there to be at hand an explicit statement of what these traditions were, for lack of which the rest of Christendom was perishing. However, the situation has now improved through the recent publication of Père Congar's monumental, scholarly and candid work *Tradition and Traditions*. He does give examples of unwritten traditions cited by the Fathers and the Scholastics, but with the following rather curious introduction:

> Perhaps it would be interesting to try to compile a list of examples which have been handed down. This is no attempt to make an inventory: Trent prudently and explicitly refused to take such a course; moreover, this is not a piece of exhaustive systematic research, but simply the result of a few notes taken while reading. In principle research along these lines should be possible. I should like to see it done one day.[9]

It is surely somewhat late in the day for such research to have remained undone. Congar then gives his list from Tertullian to Trent, which contains the following – dispensations for soldiers from wearing the military wreath, ceremonies attached to baptism and the eucharist, anniversaries on behalf of the dead and of the martyrs, the use of the sign of the cross, infant baptism, praying on the knees and facing east, the keeping of Sunday, the validity of heretical baptism, the mixing of water and wine in the chalice, election of bishops in the presence of the people, the word 'with' in the phrase 'with the Holy Spirit' (Basil), the rites of baptism, the celebration of the feasts of Easter, Ascension and Pentecost (Augustine, on the

principle that whatever is of universal usage but not found in scripture or determined by plenary councils is an apostolic tradition), the
great fasts, baptism confined to the period between Easter and Pentecost, the consecration of bishops on a Friday (Leo), the veneration
of images (John Damascene, and others after him), the essentials of
sacramental rites (Aquinas), etc.

It is possible to make distinctions with respect to such a list. Some
of the Fathers discriminate between apostolic traditions in the strict
sense and ecclesiastical traditions; others admit that an apostolic
tradition could change; only latterly has excessive appeal been made
to the forty days after Easter, of which Luke says so tantalizingly
that the Lord spent it speaking of the things pertaining to the Kingdom of God without specifying what any of these things might be.
And along with all this go frequent statements that the faith of the
church is entirely contained in scripture. But allowing for all distinctions the list is not impressive, and when placed in the solemn
context of what is necessary for salvation it strikes us as somewhat
ludicrous. Congar makes two important observations about it.
Firstly, the question came to be dominated by polemic, and 'polemic
hardens (and coarsens) intellectual positions'.[10] Whatever Protest-
ants attacked, Catholics tended to refer to an apostolic deposit, and in
this way they eventually found themselves arguing for the insuffi-
ciency of scripture and opposing tradition to it. Secondly, the periods
concerned, roughly from Tertullian to the Reformation, possessed
little or no historical sense but at the same time had an excessively
logical rather than historical conception of development. If the
Middle Ages do not contribute much and make little appeal to tradition, this is because they were concerned primarily with biblical
texts as authorities in a quasi-legal sense, and were able to arrive at
contemporary usages by an arbitrary interpretation of the text of
scripture itself.

Thus the stage was set for the Reformation and the Council of
Trent, which delivered itself in these words:

The sacred and holy ecumenical synod ... keeping this always
in view that the purity of the gospel be preserved in the church,
which gospel, promised before through the prophets in the holy
scriptures, our Lord Jesus Christ promulgated with his own
mouth, and then commanded to be preached by his apostles to

every creature as the fountain of all saving truth and moral discipline; and seeing clearly that this truth and discipline are contained in the written books and the unwritten traditions which, received by the apostles from the mouth of Christ himself, or from the apostles themselves, the Holy Spirit dictating, have come down to us transmitted as it were from hand to hand, the synod receives and venerates them with an equal affection of piety and reverence, all the books of the Old and New Testaments, as also the said traditions, as well those pertaining to faith as to mouth or by the Holy Ghost, and preserved in the Catholic morals, as having been dictated either by Christ's own word of Church by a continuous succession.

There have been a number of studies of the Council in recent years, notably that of G. H. Tavard in his *Holy Writ or Holy Church*, and he makes much of the point that the original form of words for this decree, which spoke of the truth and discipline as given '*partim*' by scripture and '*partim*' by unwritten traditions, was altered, and the '*partim* ... *partim*', which would have given a doctrine of two sources in its most rigid form, was replaced by '*et*' – the holy scriptures and the traditions, this being an echo of an agelong habit of classing the Fathers and councils with the scriptures. Congar accepts this interpretation of the Council's actions, and even asks wistfully whether it was not providentially overruled to leave the way open eventually for the more modern approach which he himself pursues. Clearly both scholars heave a sigh of relief at being rid of the necessity of subscribing to a two-source theory. Nevertheless, Congar admits, and goes out of his way to emphasize, that however it may have been at Trent itself,

> the controversialists who wrote on the subject after the council generally did so along the lines of the *partim* ... *partim* ... distinction. This was so right into the nineteenth century, and indeed even up to our own day; the texts of the magisterium which I quote in the next chapter treat Scripture and tradition as two sources of divine revelation.[11]

Further, when referring to Vatican I, and observing that in the interval the church had come more and more to be identified with the magisterium, and especially with that of the Pope, he writes,

Note too that in quoting the decree of Trent on the written books and unwritten traditions the council so cut it that it suggests the idea of two parallel and partial sources, the *partim ... partim ...* not used by Trent but generally taught by theologians since, except at Tübingen.[12]

How different is the text of Vatican II! Its tone is kerygmatic rather than dogmatic or legal. It is almost a sermon on revelation. What is said on the subject of tradition is little, and is set in the wider contexts of revelation and its source in God, the transmission of this revelation through a continuous preaching and teaching ministry, the inspiration and interpretation of scripture (here leaning heavily on the encyclical *Divino Afflante* which had brought such release to Catholic biblical scholarship), the nature of the Old and New Testaments, and the place of the Bible in the life of the church, especially for the laity. That a sore spot remained is indicated by the high drama which attended the debates on this constitution at both ends. The first draft was felt to be so unsatisfactory that, when sixty per cent voted for rejection, Pope John intervened to override the regulation that a two-thirds majority was necessary for sending it back. On the other hand it was at the intervention of Pope Paul that the sentences were included:

It is not from sacred scripture alone that the church draws her certainty about everything that has been revealed. Therefore [here echoing Trent] both sacred tradition and sacred scripture are to be accepted and venerated with the same sense of devotion and reverence.[13]

But the definitive words are in general terms. After speaking of the apostles the text continues:

But in order to keep the gospel forever whole and alive within the Church, the apostles left bishops as their successors, 'handing over their own teaching role' to them. This sacred tradition, therefore, and sacred Scripture ... are like a mirror in which the pilgrim Church on earth looks at God ... This tradition which comes from the apostles develops in the Church with the help of the Holy Spirit. For there is a growth in the understanding of the realities and the words which have been handed down ... Hence there exist a close connection and communication between sacred tradition and sacred Scripture. For both of them, flowing from the same divine wellspring, in a certain way merge into a unity, and tend toward the same end.[14]

The annotator comments that the Council here refused to decide between two views, the prevailing view since Trent that scripture and tradition may be treated separately, and that statements of revealed truth may be gathered from tradition alone, and the other view recently revived, which claims to be the pre-Tridentine teaching, and which maintains that all Christian revelation is contained in scripture, not necessarily in explicit terms sufficient to prove it, but at least by implication, and capable of being made explicit in the light of tradition.

The forms which this question of scripture and tradition has taken in the church have been determined by the particular origin and character of the Christian faith. The question may now be raised whether the historical and biblical criticism with which the church has had to learn to live in this century may not suggest that there is no way forward along these lines and in the terms in which the debate has generally been conducted. It is the temptation of the religious man to attribute too much to what speaks to him of God and brings him to God. This is wholly understandable. All our language about God is in intention the language of finality, wholeness, completeness, perfection, and what more natural than that such language should overflow into our description of what most immediately ministers the divine life and gifts? Nevertheless, it is a temptation which, if given in to, will sooner or later take its toll and lead men into untruth. Have not both sides of the debate given in to it? This question is not intended in any spirit of superiority. What Irenaeus and others achieved in desperate situations of controversy was very remarkable, and we would not have done better, if as well. But has not the debate been bedevilled by bogus claims bolstered by falsehoods, and may it not be assumed that the same Holy Spirit as inspired both scripture and tradition may also at times inspire criticism to release us from the falsehoods?

(i) Tradition. It must surely be said plainly that there are no traditions either traceable to apostles or of sufficient weight to count very much for Christian faith. Simply to list those which have been claimed as such, and to examine their pedigree so far as the evidence allows, is to make that clear. One can see the reason for the claim. Christianity is a continuing faith which embodies itself; the past is made present by a continuing action of the Spirit, and the products of the Spirit in the church have weight and authority as parts of a complex web of Christian life. To ascribe this element in Christian living to individual traditions coming from Christ and the apostles is, however, to base truth upon error, and Vatican II does not do this. It refers to 'traditions' only once, and then by quoting St Paul. Otherwise it speaks of 'tradition'. This marks the abandonment of the former view, and the substitution for it of the concept introduced into the Roman Church by Newman of an evolutionary development of doctrine. This is expressed by Vatican II in the words:

> There is a growth in the understanding of the realities and the words which have been handed down. This happens through the contemplation and study made by believers, who treasure these things in their hearts, through the intimate understanding of spiritual things they experience, and through the preaching of those who have received through episcopal succession the sure gift of truth. For as the centuries succeed one another, the Church constantly moves forward towards the fullness of divine truth until the words of God reach their complete fulfilment in her.[15]

Whether this doctrine of development will turn out to be a great boon or deadly poison it is perhaps too early to say. Certainly it spreads the concept of tradition widely over spiritual realities and delivers us from the necessity, in Congar's words, of saying about tradition what patently it is not. As denoting a continuous and living totality and an ever increasing stock of expressions of Christian faith and life, it is a very horizontal conception, and it is difficult to see how under it the truth is to be distinguished from the status quo. It does speak in the language of evolution and development which is now second nature to us, and in its faith that the church goes ever forward towards fullness it could appeal to the Epistle to the Ephesians as providing at least one way of dealing with early Christian eschatology.

(ii) Scripture. Is not this also an error, at least in the form in which it has generally been presented? Here also bogus reasons may be symptoms of a deep-seated malaise. Kurt Aland, writing on the Muratorian Canon, remarks that we can see how in the Canon's judgments 'every emerging principle on which the choice [of New Testament books] has professedly been made is expressly repudiated again in words' in the same Canon, and he concludes: 'The same state of affairs would, no doubt, become visible in all other lists of the Canon if they were not preserved in such brevity.'[16] Here again we have the case of something precious being bolstered by false claims in the effort to make it out to be more than it is or is qualified to be, and the trouble, as in the case of tradition, is the accursed mystique of 'apostolicity', from Papias and Irenaeus to Cullmann. Almost all statements of apostolic authorship made by the early Christian writers would be at least heavily queried, and probably dismissed, by a great many modern scholars, and if the word 'apostolic' is to be used of the New Testament at all it can only be in the very diffused, if not Pickwickian, sense of writings emerging we know not how, where, when or (often) for what purpose from Christian communities somewhere between roughly AD 60 and AD 130. What historical and theological distortions are involved in the emotive phrase 'the death of the last apostle'! Would it not have been better, and would it not now be better, for the church to be content with saying, 'Here are these books; we believe them to be profitable books from experience; they have come out of the lives of some of us and they express something of our faith; they are all we have, let us get on with it'? Is it, after all, obvious that the Christian church was meant to have a holy scripture in the sense of the Old Testament, which it succeeded in demoting but which it fatally took as a model? It should be granted that the written text is strong precisely where tradition is weak, and that as a fixed text it is less prone to corruption and more capable of acting as a purge, but these need be no more than debating points, as good in their way as the debating points from the other side, that it is the church which decided the canon and that scripture does not interpret itself. Is it necessary for them to be blown up into a doctrine of holy authoritative scripture? It is to be granted also that such a scripture has effected reform in the church, notably at the Reformation, though not without grave distortion, for the Reformation was nowhere more disastrous than in its belief that it had achieved a fixed doctrine of the position of scripture in the church. Is it to be assumed automatically that what scripture has done before it will necessarily do again, and that in its make-up it is fitted for this? Has not reform in our own time come from other sources, and included not only reform by the word of God but reform of the word of God? Père Bouyer may be right that the attitude of the Fathers to Bible and tradition stems from their treatment of the Bible as a whole in which we live, but this heightens the problem since, with the decisive break in the world view of the West, which is partly due to science and partly to historical studies, it is no longer possible for us to live either naturally or super-naturally in this biblical world, and how that particular past now becomes present is very problematical indeed. It is presumably a principle of scriptural interpretation that what a biblical passage means now is related to what it once meant, and a rigid doctrine of scripture will suggest that any biblical passage is, at least in principle, capable of meaning something; but we have to face the possibility that it may not now mean anything. The church is a continuing, developing community (this is the witness of tradition) and while its present life is to be in some sort of accordance with the events which gave it birth, it will not necessarily accord with any particular formulated account or understanding of those events. That the church is in history involves that its relation to the Bible is always liable to change, and the meaning of scripture will depend on other factors besides the discovery of what it once meant, important and indispensable as that may be.

(iii) Finally, it may be said that one of the results of modern studies has been to undermine the previously fixed terms scripture and tradition by approximating them to each other. Form-critical studies of the gospels and of other New Testament writings, and of the Old Testament, have shown that often the component units of writings are already in a sense traditional. They have received their shape from their use in the life of the community, have been selected for their relevance to the living interests of the church at the time, and have perhaps been moulded to those interests. In epistles are found passages with a credal, liturgical, homiletic or catechetical ring, which may have come out of a wider and richer context than that in which a particular author inserts them for his own purpose. It has always been a point on both sides of this controversy that, while the written text has a certain aura and authority as written and fixed, it does not perform its function until it once again ceases to be written and becomes oral, preached, taught, transmitted from person to person. The modern critical approach underlines this in seeing the written text as having indelibly on it the marks of its origin in the life of the community, and as being a transcript of tradition made at a certain point. It is a temptation of all men, including academics, to cry their own wares, but is there no significance at all for theology in academic procedures? What, for example, is the significance for theology and the life of the church that the scholar is so often driven outside scripture in order to make sense of it – to fetch around in II Maccabees, I Enoch and II Baruch in order to begin to make sense of such a central New Testament doctrine as resurrection? It may be that the most important contribution to theology of Rudolf Bultmann will turn out to be neither his work on form-criticism nor his programme for demythologizing, but his method in writing his *Theology of the New Testament*,[17] in which he sets out from what he believes to have been the basic kerygma of the Hellenistic church (where, of course, it is possible to dispute with him), and then interrogates each book or stratum as to how far it has continued this, how far modified it, and in what direction, and ends by using as evidence I and II Clement, Barnabas, Ignatius, Hermas and the Didache alongside the Pastorals, James, I and II Peter and Jude. If this is a legitimate method, what are its implications for the subject of scripture and tradition?

NOTES

1. M. Dufrenne, quoted by Y. Congar, *Tradition and Traditions,* Eng. trans., Burns and Oates 1966, p.264 n.1.

2. C. H. Dodd, *According to the Scriptures: the Substructure of New Testament Theology,* Nisbet 1952.

3. W. L. Knox, *The Acts of the Apostles,* Cambridge University Press 1948, p.2 n.1.

4. A. von Harnack, The *Origin of the New Testament,* Eng. trans., Williams and Norgate 1925, p.16.

5. So B. H. Streeter, *The Primitive Church,* Macmillan 1929, p.205.

6. R. P. C. Hanson, *Origen's Doctrine of Tradition,* SPCK 1954, chs. IV-V.

7. E. C. Blackman, *Marcion and his Influence,* SPCK 1948, p.94 n.1.

8. L. Bouyer, 'Holy Scripture and Tradition as Seen by the Fathers', *Eastern Churches Quarterly* VII, Supplementary Issue, 1947, pp.4f., 13ff.

9. Y. Congar, *Tradition and Traditions,* p. 48. For the list see pp.50ff.

10. *Op. cit.,* p.289.

11. G. Tavard, *Holy Writ or Holy Church*, Eng. trans., Burns and Oates 1959, pp.163f.

12. *Ibid.*, p.198.
13. 'The Dogmatic Constitution on Divine Revelation', par. 9, cited from *The Documents of Vatican II*, ed. W. J. Abbott, SJ, Geoffrey Chapman 1966, p.117.
14. *Ibid.*, pars. 7-9, pp.115-7.
15. *Ibid.*, par. 8, p.116.
16. K. Aland, *The Problem of the New Testament Canon*, Mowbray 1962, p.15.
17. R. Bultmann, *Theology of the New Testament*, 2 vols., SCM Press 1952, 1955.

2

Is 'Holy Scripture' Christian?

What kind of religion is Christianity? What kind of claims does it make for itself and for the authorities upon which it is based? There is now at hand more than one approach to such questions. Generally they have been answered from within the long tradition of Christian theology by those who have been brought up in that tradition and its appropriate disciplines. And this is very proper in so far as one can only know something from the inside. There is, however, increasingly a different approach – and in the opinion of some it ought to increase a great deal more – which would consider Christianity as a phenomenon amongst other religions, and its chief authority, the Bible, as a particular instance of the position occupied in religions by a holy book. Such was the approach of an international colloquium held in 1966 in the University of Manchester, the papers at which were published under the title *Holy Book and Holy Tradition*. I would not be qualified to attempt to make any contribution to this approach, and could only sit at the feet of those who practise it, except in so far as statements made from within the Christian tradition itself might have any bearing on wider questions of religion in general and of the place of holy scriptures in them. And it would appear that such statements could have some bearing. Thus, in the symposium referred to, the author of the paper on 'Religious Tradition and Sacred Books in Ancient Egypt' first observes that the general subject of the colloquium, the relation of scripture and tradition, is relevant in relation to non-Christian religions, since most religions possess holy books, and in some religions they function as a canon of scripture, while tradition plays ar important part in many religions, and some are totally based on it. But he then goes on to urge caution in transferring such an issue too hastily into the field of the study of non-Christian religions, continuing:

> For the subject in question obviously is a typical Christian problem. It is dubious whether we are entitled to impose these notions on other religions. It is clear that in some religions people never reflected on the question. And even if the problem in some cases actually is present, it was not thought out or formulated in any way. Actually we touch here on one of the key-questions of the methodology of the study of the history of religions. The historian of religions who is Christian by birth and who is daily handling the terminology of western scholarship, must continually ask himself whether he rightly uses certain notions in order to clarify the essence and structure of non-Christian religions.[1]

The writer then goes on to show that ancient Egyptian religion was a matter of cult, in which the secular and the holy community entirely overlapped, and that it produced no church, no doctrine and no rational theology. There were sacred authoritative texts of a kind, but they were cultic or funerary texts, and none of them had the character of a holy book in the sense of a book of fixed shape and unalterable words.

It may be concluded from the above statements that there is no direct path from some general morphology of religion to the place and character of holy books in it. There is no fixed model for the holiness of a holy book; each case has to be studied on its own and from within. How, then, is it with the Christian religion? I wish to make some observations – too few and in too little detail – on this question as it is related to (i) how the New Testament came to be regarded as holy scripture; (ii) how it came to be interpreted once it was regarded as holy scripture; and (iii) how far the New Testament as holy scripture accords with the faith to which it bears witness?

(i) How did the New Testament come to be regarded as holy scripture? Anyone who has studied what is called the history of the canon, which is the history of the process by which the New Testament writings came to have the status of holy scripture, knows how difficult it is to answer. The difficulties arise chiefly from the paucity of evidence in the vital period concerned, the first half of the second century AD, and from the often indirect character of such evidence as there is. It has often been said – and I see no reason to dissent – that there are three stages in the formation of a canon of scripture, or at any rate of the New Testament canon. The first stage is when certain writings establish themselves as authoritative on the score of their contents. What they say is felt by a sufficient number of people to be profound, convincing and particularly relevant concerning the relations of God and man – some version of Coleridge's dictum that 'what finds me testifies that it proceeds from a holy spirit'. The second stage is when writings establish themselves as authoritative on the score of their authors. X is authoritative because it has as its author a prophet, or Moses or Enoch or Homer. The third stage, which can follow from either of the other two or from a combination of them, is when writings are authoritative because they belong in an authoritative list agreed by the religious authority concerned. Authoritative now means canonical, and canonical means belonging to the canon. In the symposium referred to, S. G. F. Brandon writes somewhat dogmatically in a contrary sense. Since every known example of a holy book has had a human author or authors, and has been written in the language current in the cultural environment concerned, how, he asks, does such a writing ever come to be regarded as holy and of divine origin? He replies:

> Obviously, not because it has been self-authenticating. It is true, of course, that some Holy Books have recommended themselves as such by their intrinsic qualities; such a claim has often been advanced on behalf of the Bible by Christians or for the *Qur'ān* by Muslims, and many other instances could be cited, where the faithful are so sincerely impressed by the contents of their sacred scriptures as to think that they must, therefore, be of divine origin. However, this will always be a subsequent evaluation, and the status of a Holy Book has first to be established by some recognized spiritual authority within the community concerned. In other words, the Holy Book receives its original authentication from persons already accepted as being peculiarly endowed

with a numinous prestige and authority.[2]

However this may be with respect to other holy books, I am not so sure that this was necessarily so in the case of at least some of the New Testament writings. Though it cannot be proved, one may suspect that those most unlikely candidates for a scriptural canon, the Pauline epistles, maintained their influence, perhaps in more than one milieu, because what Paul had written seemed to make profound religious sense. As late as the time of Clement and Origen in the third century it would appear that the church at Alexandria, perhaps in distinction from other churches, was more hospitable to a greater number of Christian writings, and would have welcomed a more extensive canon, simply on the grounds that these were good books and spoke to them. This attitude can be seen behind what they have to say on the disputed question of the Epistle to the Hebrews, viz. that it is not a whit inferior to what Paul had written, as was shown by its use in so many of the churches, and that if in order to go on using it one had to say it was from an apostle, then from an apostle it must be. It is, however, the case that the criterion of self-authentication is speedily overtaken by that of authorship, and the writings are then on their way to becoming canonical on other grounds.

What brought this about in Christianity? It could be said that the Christian religion was peculiar here in that it came into being alongside an already formed conception of a holy book, the Old Testament, and as inseparable from it. In one sense this can hardly be over-emphasized. The word *gegraptai* ('it is written') and its equivalents belong to the very few technical terms in the New Testament writings, and are spread over them and govern a good deal of what they say. The translation of the *New English Bible* 'Scripture says' brings out the force. In his book *The Origin of the New Testament*,[3] Harnack listed seven forms in which early Christian writings could have been promulgated either as an appendix to, or as standing independently alongside, an already holy book, the Old Testament, and he argued that each of these seven forms had existed for a time in some areas of the early church. This is not, however, what eventually emerged, but rather a holy book now in two parts. It is conceivable that the argument could have gone the other way. For if one says that this or that had happened in fulfilment of this or that prophecy or statement of the Law, which is often said in New Testament writings, it would not be illogical to draw the conclusion that the prophecy or law in question had been rendered redundant by the fulfilment. If one uses a ladder to get to a certain place, one may legitimately kick the ladder away, providing that it is a place in which one wishes to remain. Indeed, there are sections in the New Testament, such as Paul's argument about the negative capacity of the Law, or that of the Epistle to the Hebrews for the obsolescence of priesthood and sacrifice, which could have pointed to a consequent demotion of the Old Testament from its position of a holy book of divine origin.

Even though this step was not taken, it is doubtful whether the model of the Old Testament had much influence on the early church in setting up a second holy book in combination with the first. What it did set up it placed under the double category of the Lord (= the gospels) and the apostle (= the epistles); and of these it was the latter, the apostle, which carried the greater weight, both because the Lord himself had not written anything, and because what was written about him, as well as what they were held to have written themselves, went back to the apostles. Hence the anxiety of early Christian literary critics such as Papias and his successors to show that apostolic persons were the authors of, or lay immediately behind, the gospels. Morphologically speaking, the Christian holy book owed its form and authority, and in the end its claim to divine origin, to the emergence of a figure who had some place in other religions, but his precise and central position only in Christianity, the figure of the apostle. If there was any conception which pushed the early church out of and beyond the self-authenticating position – i.e. the position of saying about its writings 'These are writings which have accompanied the Christian movement; they are the best we have and they have proved themselves' – it was the apostolic conception. The church came to believe that it possessed a New Testament scripture which was what it was because it was through and through apostolic, being the work of six apostolic men: Matthew as the author of a gospel; Peter as the author of two epistles and as looking over Mark's shoulder; John as the author of a gospel, three epistles and an apocalypse; Paul as the author of fourteen epistles and as standing behind Luke; James and Jude his brother. From the root of this conception there grew a tree with many branches and a most luxuriant foliage in which eventually all Christian birds came to nest. By the fourth century there were held to be an apostolic tradition or traditions and an apostles' creed to guide the church's belief, and an apostolic liturgy, apostolic church orders and apostolic canons to direct its worship and conduct. Nothing in fact which was not apostolic. The image of the apostle was the most powerful by which the church came to think of itself, of its character and its mission, and of the nature of its origins, its authority and its truth. And the trouble is that for us this image is almost if not entirely fantasy, and the literature which promoted it in the form of liturgy, church order, canons as well as gospels, Acts and epistles, is the literature of the imagination.

The fantasy takes two forms in accordance with the two meanings of the word 'apostolic'. By the middle of the second century Justin can write:

In fulfilment of the Old Testament prophecy that the law should go out from Jerusalem there were apostles, twelve men, and those illiterate, who by the power of God proclaimed to every race of men that they were sent by Christ to teach all the world the word of God.[4]

In pursuance of this fantasy, itself perhaps based on supposed dominical words such as those at the end of Matthew's and Luke's gospels and at the beginning of Acts, 'apostolic', deriving its force from the verb 'apostellein' meaning 'to send out', pertains to the church's world-wide mission. Eventually, as is well known, books were written to take them to all parts of the earth, whereas such little evidence as we have suggests that, with the exception of Peter, they remained in Jerusalem exercising their function of being the Twelve. The second form of the fantasy can be seen perhaps fifty years earlier than Justin, when Clement of Rome can write:

The apostles received the gospel for us from the Lord Jesus. Jesus Christ was sent from God. Thus Christ is from God and the apostles are from Christ. In both instances the orderly procedure proceeds from God's will ... and the apostles after preaching in country and city appointed their first converts to be bishops and deacons of future believers ... And this was no novelty, since

Scripture says, 'I will appoint your bishops in righteousness and your deacons in faith.'[5]

From this develops the meaning of 'apostolic' which is derived not from the verb but from the noun 'apostle', and which applies not to mission or evangelism but to office, zeal, wisdom, words, writing or doctrine. The fantasy in this form is of the apostle as the immediate recipient from the Lord, and so as the original and sure basis of the church and its faith. The image is of the church's origination from an unfailing source in a divine history, and of its pedigree – an image not of what it is for, as in the missionary understanding, but of what it is from. And this begets its own type of legend, that of the so-called 'apostolic age', from which all later ages must trace their descent. This age depends on the physical presence for the church of those who through their special relation to Christ are apostles. As the oldest of them reaches his end the church, as it were, waits in suspended animation. He breathes his last; a gong sounds throughout the Christian world. The apostolic age is over, and the sub-apostolic age has begun. That this is not pure caricature may be seen from the power exercised until very recently in both Protestant and Catholic circles by the highly emotive phrase 'the death of the last apostle' to underline the significance of the New Testament as a holy book.

Modern scholarship has not been without its own way of refurbishing the image. Perhaps the most notable example has been Karl Rengstorf's influential article on '*Apostolos*' in Kittel's *Wörterbuch zum Neuen Testament*. The argument runs as follows. The notion of apostle rests on the precise Jewish background of the *shaliach*, a legal arrangement by which one who was sent on a task had a power of attorney, expressed in the dictum 'he who is sent by a man is as the man who sends him'. When the task is religious this arrangement can take on a religious tone. The central idea is that of authorized agency, with emphasis on the one who authorizes. This is to be taken back into the mind of Jesus, as when he says 'He who receives you receives me', and there are no adequate grounds for doubting Luke's statement that 'He chose twelve, whom he named apostles'. The originally limited task during the period of Jesus' earthly ministry was not, however, simply continued on into the post-resurrection period. It was renewed by the resurrection appearances; and though not all witnesses of the resurrection were apostles, it was through the apostles as witnesses to the resurrection and their personal commission that the church was established as a preaching community. The new situation turned them into missionaries, and it is the missionary element which now stamps apostleship and differentiates it from the Jewish institution of the *shaliach*. The appointment is for the period between Easter and the unknown date of the parousia, and it was limited to the first generation. It could not become a permanent office in the church. Since the scope of the risen Lord was universal, so was the scope of the apostolic office.

This is the critical account which claims to establish apostleship on bases which are not romantic nor fantastic, but which are linguistically, historically and theologically controlled. It would require too much detail to examine this thesis fully. It is, however, vulnerable at its chief points. It is by no means clear that the Jewish institution stands immediately behind the Christian apostle, or even that there is firm evidence for its existence at the time. In view of the strong missionary sense in the majority of instances of the word 'apostle' in the New Testament (seventy out of eighty-one are found in Paul and Luke-Acts) it would be a less tortuous thesis to suppose that 'apostle' was a noun precipitated by the verb 'to send out' in its missionary sense than to suppose that the new situation after the resurrection imparted a fresh sense to the concept of *shaliach*, which sense then took over. The historico-theological point whether the idea of the apostle can be taken back into the life of Jesus subdivides into a number of questions. Did he conceive of the choice of the twelve as in any sense constituting an apostolate? Did he use the term of them? Did he intend a universal mission before, or even after, the resurrection? There is a clear affirmative answer to these questions, and to all of them at once, only in the Lucan writings, as there is also there the germ of the idea of the apostles as the guarantors of the events of the gospel history. It is a tenable hypothesis that this is all the creation of that type of Christianity which finds expression in the Lucan writings. These are, indeed, all complex questions, but in this context one is not so much concerned with whether they can be satisfactorily answered as with the fact that they can on the evidence be raised at all. For this fact that they can be raised at all is bound to mean that the image of the apostle is to a greater or less extent a blurred image, and the adjective 'apostolic' comes to be used in an increasingly Pickwickian sense. One might ask the question, 'What if anything is being said about a Christian writing, practice or institution over and above its intrinsic worth by calling it "apostolic"?' Should books be written with titles such as 'The Apostolic Age' or 'The Sub-Apostolic Age'?

The point may be illustrated by reference to Oscar Cullmann's book, *Salvation in History*.[6] Before proceeding to complete a trilogy by adding to his previous two works *Christ and Time* and *The Christology of the New Testament*[7] a study of eschatology, he has turned aside to write this book in view of the theological debate on the continent between those who interpret the Christian gospel primarily in existential terms and those who do not, to meet criticisms of his previous works and to consolidate their positions. As he sees it, the one, overall, necessary, normative and determinative conception is that of *Heilsgeschichte*. That is, Christianity is basically a series of events, the connection between which is not made on any historical principle as such, but by an association which makes the events divine revelation about history. To be a Christian is to be in some way aligned with these events. In pursuit of this view he is led to state categorically that the apostolic nature of the canon must be upheld at all costs. The limitation of salvation history, i.e. the fact that it comes to a decisive point in Christ and in what he gives rise to,

> amounts to the fixing of the canon. It seems to me impossible to justify the canon apart from salvation history, and it is not by accident that its justification is inevitably questioned whenever salvation history is rejected.

And then in a somewhat emotionally charged passage:

> The demand to be 'honest' in the area of Christian thought is raised with special emphasis today. Among other things the question must also be raised whether in all honesty we may really lay the Bible upon our altars if we reject what makes these books in particular into the 'Bible', namely, salvation history.[8]

What Cullmann means here is something quite precise. The canon is apostolic in the sense that it reproduces the eyewitness of the apostles, and the apostles' eyewitness is more important than that of all other biblical witnesses because it relates to the decisive events, and in this way indirectly guarantees the revelation to all the previous witnesses and marks the end of all the preceding history of interpretation. He is thus led to speak of 'the time of the apostles', and to say of the Twelve that they hold a unique position as those who as well as being witnesses of the resurrection were also disciples of the incarnate Lord, in that they had to guarantee the continuity between the events and the kerygma given them.[9] But honesty may cut more ways than one; and what is disturbing about this passage quoted above is not so much the pistol at the head with the threat 'Believe in *Heilsgeschichte* [which I do not] or perish', as the assertion that one cannot honestly place the Bible upon the altar unless one is prepared to affirm that its quality of Bible is established by its apostolic character. For the apostolic concept has been more responsible than most for, one would not say dishonesty (for moral judgments had better be eschewed in this matter), but for fantasy. Will any amount of refurbishing restore the apostolic image to be the *raison d'être* of the New Testament as holy book? Can we only begin to see what the New Testament is when the fantasy has been swept away?

(ii) How did the New Testament come to be interpreted once it had become holy book? How did it play its part when it had passed both beyond the position of being authoritative because it was self-authenticating and beyond the position of being authoritative because it was an apostolic production, and had come to belong to the category of scripture? One of the consequences of this happening was that oral tradition ceased to accompany what had been written, and subsequently died out. Its place and function were now taken by exegesis or interpretation of the holy book. And what is troubling here is the comparative futility of so much Christian exegesis down the ages. By this it is not meant to pass judgment in some superior and arrogant fashion on the ways in which scripture may have been misapplied by the preacher or teacher in making his point. We would not in any case be in a position to do this, since the greater part of Christian exposition has not come down to us, and much of what has come down has done so because it belonged to a great figure who was important for other reasons than his exegesis. And if some piece of exposition struck us as very strange, that might be to its credit. The expositor in this way might have made a passage of scripture speak very directly to his audience, and if we knew more about the situation of the audience we might see how much this was the case. What is at issue here is, rather, the official canons and methods of interpretation which grew up by reason of the New Testament's being a holy book; and above all the typological and allegorical methods, which were dominant until comparatively recently. This is, of course, a very long story, and in attempting to summarize it I would like to make a lengthy reference to another contribution to the symposium referred to above, that of B. Moeller, who is writing on the Middle Ages and Luther.[10] Some of the points which Moeller makes are as follows. He observes that for the Middle Ages truth was a gift of overpowering fullness and grandeur, and it was held to have been given to man in advance. This is why they were so prone to issuing forgeries; it was to assert that what had been discovered had really always existed. Truth lay in the past, and the word 'modern' was a pejorative term. The place where truth was to be found was primarily in the writings of antiquity, especially the holy book, the Bible. Here God had given men access to the knowledge of how they had been created, what they had to do, and what lay before them and the world. The way to this truth was the exposition of these writings, which were characterized on the one hand by their divine authority and on the other by their strangeness, the latter being something new in the attitude to antiquity. Hence a new understanding of the Bible began in the Middle Ages. One could track down the truth in these texts if one used the right exegetical method. This, says Moeller, had nothing to do with a historical attitude in our sense; it could best be called a figurative interpretation, or a typological interpretation such as is already found in the early church and within the New Testament itself. It conveyed not only a strong sense of the unity of truth through one event prefiguring another, but 'the wonderful spiritual sense, which the exegete found, and in which it became visible beyond and above the reality of the concealed plan of God', a sense which 'went far beyond the framework of exegesis of Scripture as such', and expressed itself above all in pictorial art.[11] This was the symbolic element in interpretation. But these were not the only ways for laying bare scripture, and for the reason – and this is the crucial issue – that there was a hiatus at the critical point.

> If it really was God Himself who spoke to man in Holy Scripture, one could not be content with the explanation of specific parts of the book as holy truth. Rather it had to be defended as authoritative in its entirety and in every detail.[12]

And it was the allegorical method which performed this service, for it is a principle of allegorical exegesis that any text has to fit into the whole and with every other part. For Origen, who was its first major Christian exponent, failure to maintain a consistent harmony of interpretation from beginning to end was a mark of heresy; and it is understandable that some of the earliest Christian allegorists were the Gnostics, since they possessed a single system of thought, and the text had to fit the system at all points. As Moeller remarks, in contrast with the figurative interpretation allegorizing was not specifically Christian. 'The Alexandrian Church fathers, who made it firm in the Church, had prototypes in the profane exegesis of Homer and Virgil, and in the philosophical hellenistic exposition of the Old Testament.'[13] From these beginnings it was built into the medieval four-fold interpretation of scripture, the rules for which were first laid down by the monk John Cassian in the fifth century. But, as Moeller interestingly observes, whereas allegorizing in respect of pagan writers had something of a demythologizing function, i.e. it made the gods and their behaviour and the incongruities in divine things somehow palatable and meaningful, in the case of the Christian scriptures it was different, since it was now used above all to demonstrate the axiom of 'the completely Augustinian sentence *"Nihil est in divina scriptura, quod non pertineat ad ecclesiam"* ',[14] and so to uphold the divinity and unity of the writings as holy scripture in all their parts. Thus it could be said that writings, whether pagan or Christian, become casualties to allegorizing as a direct consequence of their coming to be regarded as together constituting holy writ. 'Become casualties' is, of course, a loaded expression, but is any other possible for us who are bound to reject the method as a kind of saving of the appearances? From the angle of a historical critical approach it is only by repudiating the method that one can begin to see what the New Testament writings are about. If this is so, the question is inescapable whether the approach which we repudiate is nevertheless one which cannot but arise once the writings have come to belong to the category of holy book. This is what was meant above by the comparative futility of much Christian exegesis.

That we are left here with a host of problems is evident from the way in which the question of 'hermeneutics', which is only another word for exegesis or interpretation, has recently thrust its way into the forefront of theological discussion. To participate in this discussion is soon to be made aware of the difficulties it entails. The oft quoted judgment in ecumenical circles that despite their divisions at other levels the churches all have the Bible in common refers, of course, to an empirical fact, but it turns out to be a comparatively superficial fact. For as soon as a group gets down to the task of exegesis and looks for principles of interpretation it becomes apparent that the differences of approach are great, sometimes so great that it might not be the same book that they are all studying, and it begins to appear problematical whether there are any agreed principles beyond the scholarly techniques of study which have now become common property. Beyond those techniques there generally emerges some kind of dogma about a holy book, or about God himself, such as to determine the approach. An example is the typological exegesis which has undergone something of a revival in recent years. There are two questions involved here. The first is factual. If a New Testament writer thought and wrote typologically – that is, if he thought and wrote in such a way as to present the life and death of Jesus as following a pattern of significant action already laid down in the Old Testament, the Exodus say, or the career of Moses – then this is how he thought and wrote, and to neglect the fact would be to disregard something essential for a proper exegesis of that writer. The dispute would then be whether he does so think and write, or to what extent he does so, or whether this is being read into his work. But, beyond that, typological exegesis rests upon a dogma about God, which, like other dogmas, has to run the gauntlet as to whether it can establish itself, and can do so on more than a biblical basis. When Plato said 'God always geometrizes' he made a statement about God which was based on deduction from what seemed to him the character of existence. It was open to criticism as being based on limited observation and as not taking sufficiently into account the non-geometrical aspects of life. Typology implies the statement that God, unlike history, repeats himself, or repeats himself significantly at least once. This is also open to examination, and perhaps to the suspicion that it results from an over-preoccupation of the Israelites with the significance of their own historical experience. Or again, there is the problem, which is very soon encountered in hermeneutics, of the unity and diversity of the New Testament. The diversity has been made apparent by historical criticism. The unity is a problem only because of the dogma of a holy book. For why should it be supposed that these writings should exhibit a unity other than that which they possess through emerging from communities which had a good deal of belief and practice in common, except on the supposition that as holy book they must reflect more obviously and immediately the unity of God himself and of the truth?

(iii) How far does the concept of the holy book accord with the faith to which the New Testament bears witness? Here one can only be tentative. The question is connected with what is called the secularization of Christianity. This can take more than one form, and is something of a theological fashion. As such it has to be scrutinized with particular care. Yet there may well be something in it which is more than an accommodation to the spirit of the age. Could it not be said that it was of the essence of the Christian gospel in its earliest period that it abolished the category of the holy except as applied to God himself (and perhaps to the community which was in living touch with him)? One thinks, for example, of the comparative secularity of the synoptic gospel picture of one who worked in Galilee and not in the holy city, who was rejected by Jerusalem and perhaps rejected it, who performed his acts of salvation in relation to the concrete ills of human beings, and who proclaimed the rule of God in terms largely free from the cultic or ecclesiastical. Or, from a different angle, one thinks of Paul's passionate refusal of the sacral badge of circumcision as a *sine qua non* of salvation, and his demotion of the sacred law to at least a secondary place and to a largely negative function (though admittedly by setting one part of scripture against another), by which he initiated a discussion about the place of the Old Testament scripture in the church which for a time at least could have had more than one conclusion, and which was perhaps foreclosed too easily and too soon. Or from a different angle still there is the Epistle to the Hebrews. To whom this was written and for what precise purpose, remain riddles, but it is a tenable hypothesis that the author's theme that Christians are in possession of the inner truth of temple, priesthood and sacrifice because they have these things in a heavenly mode in Christ, derives some of its point from his readers living in a world where religion was indissolubly bound up with sacred rites (and, if Orphic, with sacred writings), and where the natural questions to ask of any-one who professed a religion were 'Where are your holy places?', 'Where is your priesthood?', 'Where are your rites?', and 'Where are your holy books?' Is it significant that Christianity was without a holy land or centre until in the fourth century Constantine's wife popularized tours to the holy places and the Bishop of Jerusalem cashed in with splendid liturgies, or until later, and perhaps follow-ing a hint already dropped in the Lucan writings, there was a most forceful sacralization of the secular, and the centre was located at Rome?

If there is anything in what is called the secular element in Chris-tianity (and we have been frequently reminded that one of the earliest charges against Christians was that they were atheists, mean-ing that they did not fit into any recognized religious pattern), does a holy book fit into this or not? If it was the case that religious models, and especially the Old Testament, were in the end too much for Christianity, so that a time came when it was no longer possible to say, 'These are writings which have belonged from the first to our movement, they are the best we have and they have recommen-ded themselves', and one could only say 'This is holy scripture', does it follow that this is of the nature of the case, and that the church has always to think in this way? In his contribution to the sym-posium already mentioned Geo. Widengren makes an observation about Islam which could provide an analogy. He notes that in the *Qur'ān* the adversaries of the Prophet demand of him two signs to show himself the true bearer of revelation – that he should mount to heaven, and that he should bring down a book which they can read. The prophet refuses the demand with the statement: 'Say: Glory be to my Lord! Am I but a man, an Apostle?' Yet despite this there grew up a whole literature describing the prophet doing precisely these two things – his ascension to God and his receiving the *Qur'ān* at the hands of God – so that, in Widengren's words, 'the old pattern of the Ancient Near East has triumphed over the historical truth'.[15]

The question broached in this chapter brings along with it all manner of other highly important questions. If Cullmann is right it involves the nature of Christianity itself. Is Christianity an authoritative religion, and if so what kind of authority is indigenous to it? What kind of divine truth does it profess to have and to convey, and in what form does it convey it? What kind of certainty does it have and what kind of ambiguity? They are broached here only with relation to the three points of the supposed apostolic origin of the New Testament, of the kind of exegesis which the concept of a holy book inevitably tends to produce, and of the genius of Christianity, if one might call it that, to secularize the sacred. This is what is meant by the chapter's perhaps foolish title.

NOTES

1. C. J. Bleeker, 'Religious Tradition and Sacred Books in Ancient Egypt', in *Holy Book and Holy Tradition*, ed. F. F. Bruce and E. G. Rupp, Manchester University Press 1968, p.21.

2. S. G. F. Brandon, 'The Holy Book, the Holy Tradition and the Holy Ikon', *op. cit.*, p.3.

3. A. von Harnack, *The Origin of the New Testament*, 1925, Appendix II, pp.169ff.

4. Justin, I *Apology* 39.

5. I Clement 42, citing Isa. 60.17 in a form otherwise unknown.

6. *Salvation in History*, Eng. trans., SCM Press 1967.

7. *Christ and Time*, Eng. trans., rev. ed., SCM Press 1962; *The Christology of the New Testament*, Eng. trans., 2nd ed., SCM Press 1963.

8. *Salvation in History*, pp.294, 298.

9. *Ibid.*, pp.102f.

10. B. Moeller, 'Scripure, Tradition and Sacrament in the Middle Ages and in Luther', *Holy Book and Holy Tradition*, pp.113ff.

11. *Ibid.*, p.118.

12. *Ibid.*, p.119.

13. *Ibid.*, p.120.

14. *Ibid.*

15. Geo. Widengren, 'Holy Book and Holy Tradition in Islam', *op. cit.*, p.219.

3

Should the New Testament
be taught to Children

This question in comparison with the previous one might appear to
be flippant. But it is not intended to be so, and indeed, is not so. The
critical and analytical study of the Bible may begin, and may continue for some time, as an academic pursuit, but sooner or later it
comes to bear on the practitioner who may be occupied with the
Bible in various circumstances and at various levels as an instrument
of teaching. There is a two-way process here. Theology exists in the
first and in the last resort for the church. It would not exist at all did
not the church exist as an entity in the world. However much it may
and must, where possible, do its work within the university faculties
according to the most rigorous standards of scholarship available –
and on this score it does not have much to be ashamed of; indeed
it has sometimes led the way – it must in the end come out and face
the church. This applies to some extent to other disciplines also.
There are times when the scientist feels that he is accountable to
society and that he must have a conscience about what is done with
his work. But for the theologian this has always to be so, which
makes him a somewhat ambiguous figure who is subject to peculiar
tensions. Sooner or later he must draw out and bear to the governor
of the feast, and the value and validity of his work are tested in this
way. He is not concerned simply with his own private interests. But
it goes the other way also. The church exists in the world out of its
theology, that is, out of its understanding of the world and of human
life in it in their relation to God and his word – which is the literal
meaning of the word theology. It must, therefore, be prepared to
listen to its theologians, however much it may disapprove of them.

As Käsemann observes, the piety of the pious cannot be allowed to have the last word, if only because the piety of the pious seems so often to be occupying some kind of halfway house between the basic formulations – be they those of the Middle Ages or of the Reformation – and the present day without very much understanding of either. And piety cannot have the last word with the Bible because it does not turn out to be that kind of book; it does not speak immediately and directly to the present time as though two thousand years did not lie between.[1]

But a considerable part of this problem does not lie within the immediate sphere of the churches but of the schools. It is often said that the church is now in a missionary situation, and what that means can be spelt out in more ways than one. Sometimes the statement is little more than a groan of disquiet about we know not what; sometimes a ground for knocking whatever aspects of the establishment we may not like. But it can go very deep, and if it is true it is true in a new sense. Hitherto the missionary situation facing the church has been, whatever its difficulties, one in which the tide was still running the way of Christianity as it lapped round new peoples, emerging nations and fresh thought. But now the tide is ebbing, not only in the established existence of some form of Marxism as the common faith of large areas of the world, or in the rise of independent nations who repudiate Christianity along with Western imperialism, but nearer home with the slow emergence within the framework of so-called Christian societies of alternative views of life to Christianity, which can at times coagulate and find themselves a name, as, for example, Humanism. The missionary situation involves something far more complex than questions whether the church will prove sufficiently mobile to adapt its inheritance, its organization or its ministry in time. It is concerned with thought, and with the attitudes to life with which the young come to adulthood. It is therefore concerned not primarily with the church but with the schools, as it is plainly the school which is more responsible than any other single agency, including in most cases now the family, in developing these attitudes. In what state of mind so far as Christian belief is concerned will the church find the young when they leave school?

I have no particular qualifications for discussing this question, except that as chaplain and lecturer in a Teacher Training College

I once had the privilege of entrée into, and membership of, the teaching world, which is a world very much on its own, with its own particular standards and techniques, and where there is often an enthusiasm and idealism which is seldom found elsewhere. Knowing little about educational theory and practice one received far more than one gave, but since one's subject was divinity one became acutely aware that a theological battle was being fought less over the bodies of the clergy and their dwindling but still voluntary congregations than over the bodies of the teachers and their large but compulsory audiences; and that the battle was being lost. The Education Act providing for the teaching of scripture in schools was a moment in the long and complex struggle in English society to discover how agnostic its corporate soul really is. It represented the unwillingness of a majority to pronounce openly that England was no longer a Christian society. Since this was a decision of adults not about their own beliefs, but about their children, who were not to be denied the foundations of a religious belief and practice which in many cases they themselves did not share, there was bound to be a large measure of unreality about it, and it thereby risked putting Bible teaching on the same level as other features in society which could be reckoned as relics of Christianity, and as flotsam left by the receding tide. And there has been continuing opposition to it, especially more recently, from those who have found a common title in humanism, and who therefore object to a position in which those who hold a liberal democratic outlook on man and certain more or less agreed ethical views should have, so far as the schools are concerned, to be assembled under the Christian umbrella. But there it is. And into the execution of the Act has gone a vast amount of thought and devotion. Since, naturally, any denominational theology was excluded, the syllabus was largely confined to the Bible in the belief – illusory as it turns out in the light of the discussion on hermeneutics – that all Christians have this in common and are in a large measure agreed over it, though it was a new feature that this agreement was held to include the Apostles' Creed. Education Authorities set themselves to produce syllabuses, some of which were of the highest order. The assistance of the best theologians in the land was sought and given. But the result has been almost nil, nil, or in some cases worse than nil. From the missionary situation of the church, as it contemplates the young leaving school and moving theoretically into its orbit as potential adult Christians, the result has not been that society, in the person of the schools, has produced a considerable number of those who have been given the foundations of a Christian understanding of life. For the most part scripture teaching falls off them as though it had never been, except that in some instances it has immunized them against at any rate the church, and probably against Christianity, which they believe they have seen through. An obvious immediate explanation for this is that the Bible has been taught outside the context of the worship and living membership of the church where it belongs, and from which and to which it speaks, to children whose parents – the other formative influence outside the school – do not for the most part worship and are not living members of the church. This is the agony of the conscientious teacher of the large but compulsory congregation. But this is not the whole story. For the English Public Schools, which are close knit communities with a chapel and worship at the centre – though again the worship of the children of largely non-worshipping parents – show an equally poor return. A recent survey by a university chaplain showed a defection rate from Christian belief and worship in first-year undergraduates of over ninety per cent.

More recently there have been serious second thoughts about all this, primarily in the work of Ronald Goldman and others. Again, I am not qualified to discuss this technically, but it is, I think, significant that the queries have come not from the theological side but from that of educational and psychological research, and that the contention is that this form of scriptural instruction deals in concepts which do not correspond with the child's experience of life, and aims at putting an old head on young shoulders. This contention may be seen as an indication of a general truth applicable over the whole field. I would like to claim quite simply that the New Testament ought not to be taught to children because it is a book for adults and crystallizes the religious experience of adults, and that if taught to children it is either talking about experience which is beyond what they have or ought to have, or it is disembowelled in various ways in an attempt to bring it within what is supposed to be their experience. This is, of course, a general statement, but it may be defended even in its rough and ready terms. By adult is meant a human being who is of necessity faced with responsibility, and who has to make decisions as a result of that responsibility. By child is meant a human being who is not, or who is very little, burdened with responsibility, and who ought not to be so burdened. The family, the school and society aim at protecting the child from such responsibility, and one of the functions of the parent, or of whoever stands *in loco parentis*, is to act as a cushion between the child and the tragedy of life, and to filter experience through to the child as it is able to receive it. Life being a very untidy affair, it never quite happens like this; some adults do not grow up, and the protective screen for children is rudely shattered by the irruption of events beyond their capacities to absorb. But by and large the distinction stands.

I would wish to maintain that in these terms the New Testament is throughout a thoroughly adult book, is so by the circumstances of its origins and of the origins of Christianity, and has been shown to be so by historical criticism. To be more specific, the Christian gospel in its manifold forms, from the beatitudes to the book of Revelation, is addressed to those who know what responsibility is, who have been battered about by it, who know something of what it means to be at the end of one's tether, or whose self-confidence which keeps this battering at bay has first to be punctured. This is immediately evident in the epistles, and especially in the epistles of Paul, who is perhaps the only person to stand out with any clarity at all in the New Testament. But there are two ways in which Paul can be made to stand out. The first is by paying careful attention to his letters, through which it has been said he becomes better known to us than any other figure in the acient world except Cicero. There is evidence that their original recipients found them difficult, and the so-called Second Epistle of Peter is evidence that they were found very difficult later on. The second is by concentrating on the presentation in heroic mould which Luke gives in the second half of Acts, when he takes Paul as the test case of his own understanding of what Christianity is. Paul for the children is inevitably some form of the latter; and if the child ever comes to study theology at the university level it proves to be one of the most difficult things from which to detach him. But in the view of many Pauline scholars, to treat the secondary source, Acts, as the primary source for Paul is to commit a methodological *faux pas*. For there are considerable differences between the Paul of the epistles and the Paul of Acts both in relation to the mission and to doctrine. So far as one can gather from the authentic Pauline letters his view of his mission was that God had reversed the predestined order of salvation, and that in the double mission which he shared with Peter and his companions it was that to the Gentiles which was to precede and even bring about the salvation of Israel, and that he, Paul, and his companions, had the burden of evangelizing the whole Gentile world representatively before the coming of Christ. This was a monstrous conception, and some of the adjustments made in the picture of Paul by the later deutero-Pauline writings were brought about by its failure, and by the fact that subsequently, when apocalyptic thought had died, it was no longer even comprehensible. To this time belongs Luke, for whom Paul is the missionary *par excellence* in the successful progress of the gospel and the church by stages, until, with his arrival at Rome, it reaches the centre of the world. Thus the children's lessons on Paul become inevitably lessons in some kind of geography-cum-ancient history, which could only be justified if it was a necessary background for a later study of the Paul of the Pauline epistles, which it is not. Paul is left hanging in the air as an illegitimate subject and an unreal figure, the real motives of whose actions and movements do not appear. For if one's aim is to teach ancient geography and ancient history it is not evident that Paul qualifies for this rather than Julius Caesar or Socrates. There is no justification for selecting Paul's particular geography and his history except that he is part of the New Testament; and there is no justification for teaching about Paul in the context of the New Testament unless one proceeds from his epistles, which one does not because they are too adult. Or in the matter of doctrine. As is well known, part of what made Paul himself tick, and of what has made him an explosive force in the church, is his doctrine of justification by faith. But no one in his senses attempts to teach this to children. In the English scene it is often only taught to adults when its edge has first been blunted by caricaturing 'the Law' as a large collection of narrow prohibitions which would find difficult to take seriously anyhow. But this is not what Paul is talking about, as we can see if for the archaic term 'the Law' we were to substitute 'morality', which is what Paul means by it, and divine morality to boot. In opposition to those who claimed that a Gentile must embrace the whole of this divine morality if he is to attain the salvation upon which he has only started by faith in Christ, Paul is led to assert that the function of morality, even of

God's Old Testament morality, is at best positive-negative, and in actuality negative. It is positive in that apart from the Law I would not know God's mind and will, but in relation to conditions as they are it is negative. Its function is to bring to light what sin is without any capacity to deal with the situation which it has brought to light. Its nature is death-dealing and it kills; it brings men to the position where they may receive God's free grace. This represents Paul's great contribution to the adult world of the Christian gospel; one might say to the history of ethics. It is daring and breath-taking, and Paul himself is well aware that he is walking on a knife edge and is in danger of toppling over into the antinomianism of some of his later followers, or into the position which his opponents accused him of holding, that we may sin that grace may abound. This sophisticated doctrine cannot of course be taught to children, whose morality, if it has to be biblical at all, is very properly that of the book which is, perhaps, the quintessence of the Old Testament, viz. Deuteronomy, with its variations on the theme: 'If you are good you will be happy, and if you are bad you will not, because you are living in a world which is God's world.'

There is no need to go into detail with respect to the rest of the non-gospel literature in the New Testament – the deutero-Pauline letters, Hebrews, First and Second Peter and Revelation, since the syllabus seldom uses these writings as wholes for source material, but if it uses them at all takes passages from them to fill out a theme, which is in itself a doubtfully legitimate procedure, and something of a confession of defeat. So we come to the gospels, where there is still a lingering sense that we can by-pass theology and arrive at a core of biblical Christianity which is essentially simple and straightforward. But the idea that the gospel in the gospels is simple is a nineteenth-century heresy, and much damage has been done in the circles who still entertain it by the phrase 'simple Galilean fishermen'. For not only does the New Testament as a whole, and the gospels in particular, have little if anything to do with Galilean fishermen (if they were originally concerned with handing on the oral tradition out of which the gospels were made, they already lie a long way in the background by the time the evangelists are handling it), but one can counter with the question 'How simple was a Galilean fisherman?' In relation to almost everything that modern children come to know so much about – mathematics, physics, history, geography, etc. – he was a non-starter. But in one respect he was likely to be far ahead of them, for he had drunk in with his mother's milk one of the richest and most complex religious traditions the world has ever seen, the Jewish, whereas here even the sixth-former, in the absence of a strong religious or philosophical tradition, is something of a non-starter.

At this point the biblical critic has made things hard for the teacher. The Fourth Gospel in any case presents a problem of considerable complexity, and needs to be treated on its own. It is grossly mishandled when sections are taken out of it to fill in gaps left by the synoptists. This is a book with a most elusive combination of simplicity and profundity. It has somehow to be put on the background of the crisis hinted at in the First Epistle of John, where there appears to be a conflict over what may have been the earliest problem concerning the person of Christ, viz. whether he was really a man at all. How complex this thought background might be can be seen from one of the greatest books of our time on the subject, C. H. Dodd's *The Interpretation of the Fourth Gospel*,[2] with its introductory chapters on the Old Testament, rabbinic thought, the Gnostics, the Hermetic literature and Philo as supplying possible ingredients for it (and some would now want to add the Qumran scrolls). If this gospel is to be taught at all, it has to be at a late stage, and in connection with the question which it poses of the nature of religious language and its relation to symbolism. So we come to the synoptic gospels, the teacher's bastion out of which he seldom ventures except for the Paul of Acts. Two things have happened here which make his work difficult. In the first place, as the form critics have been saying *ad nauseam*, the synoptic material when properly assessed, that is when assessed according to its pericopal or unit form, allows no possibility of a life of Jesus. This is difficult enough for the preacher, since it means that in order to expound the unit he has to envisage it as having assumed the form it has because it bore particularly on some aspect of the gospel message in general, as that message was understood in the light of the Easter faith and the Spirit. The acts and words of Jesus are the vehicles of that message. This makes heavy demands on the preacher's exegesis, but he is at least preaching in a context which makes this feasible, as he is faced with an adult believing congregation which is assembled in the light of the Easter faith, and the creed which it is professing may provide the matrix for the unit which is to be expounded. But with the teacher this is not so. He is not faced with such a congregation engaged in the act of Christian worship; he is in the classroom, where the natural thing is to teach a continuous history. The preacher does not have to say to his congregation 'Come again next week and I will tell you what happened next and why'; but the teacher who is engaged with the syllabus and the periods which are to follow is almost impelled to this, and is thus impelled to go against the nature of the material he is handling.

In the second place biblical criticism has shown that much of the material in the synoptic gospels, and of that which holds them together, does not come directly from the Old Testament, but from apocalyptic, that rather strange development of thought which took place in the period between the Old and New Testaments. There is, of course, a close connection between the Old and New Testaments both factually and historically and also in the sphere of thought. But if one were to put together the concepts of the kingdom of God (with its synonym 'the coming age') and of the Son of man, miracles (and especially the exorcism of demons) and parables, these would constitute a considerable part of the material which is central to the synoptic gospels, and none of it derives directly from the Old Testament. The term 'the kingdom of God' does not appear as such in the Old Testament, and the phraseology which goes with it has only just begun to appear in the latest of its books, Second Zechariah and Daniel. The title 'the Son of man' does not appear as such in the Old Testament, and the literature about this important but elusive term, and about its relation to the vision in Daniel 7, is enormous and arrives at no agreed conclusion. There is no demonology in the Old Testament to assist our understanding of Jesus' acts of power or his own interpretation of them. Parables in the gospel sense are very rare in the Old Testament, and their immediate background is the exegetical methods of the rabbis. Now apocalyptic is a difficult, even weird phenomenon. It is cosmological, mythological, and on the whole governed by pessimism. Compared with the apocalyptists the Old Testament prophets are frequently optimistic; they believe that the situation could be mended if men were to repent in response to the threat of divine judgment. But apocalyptists tend to believe that evil is too deep seated to allow men to repent in this way, and that only a pure act of God can deal with the situation, and that act one of cosmic proportions involving a universal judgment, resurrection and a new creation of the world. But what about the parables? Surely here we are safe from irreverent hands? So it is thought, with the result that at a certain stage divinity tends to become such a constant diet of parables that it achieves a different result from that intended, since it is bound to make at least the better children sick through overeating. But we are not safe here. For some of the parables are about this kingdom of God and this Son of man; and even when they are not they frequently exhibit the clearest examples of modification or of multiple modifications of an original tradition in order to make it speak to the conditions not of those who originally heard, but of those attempting to live the Christian life and hold the post-Easter faith in circumstances which the original parables did not envisage. Is not one of the great books on the parables in our time that of J. Jeremias, who with great technical skill, like that of a surgeon with his scalpel, removes one layer after another until he gets back to Jesus (and is perhaps too confident in some cases that he has done so)? And is not one of the most difficult passages in the New Testament, past which the children must be hurried with averted eyes, that in Mark's Gospel, copied by Matthew and Luke, which declares that parables are for the outsider, so that seeing he may not perceive and hearing he may not understand? Where then is the simplicity of the gospel?

On these grounds it may be maintained that the New Testament is not fitted for children, and does not speak to their needs. If one is allowed to appeal to the example of Jesus one might note that he is nowhere represented as teaching children – nor are his disciples – and that all that he is represented as doing is blessing them and returning them to their mothers, where in those days they belonged. This would seem to be an important factor in the missionary situation as it actually is, which successive manoeuvres in the religious educational field only serve to mask rather than to face, because it is still hoped that with respect to the Bible the children will somehow save the day. Perhaps the single largest counter factor to Christianity in our society as it has developed is the presence of so many young men and women who, as the products of this system, not only are not ready to consider Christianity as a real option, but have been, perhaps permanently, immunized against it as something which has already been all heard before and seen through. It is not something to grow into, but something already grown out of. The retort is, of course, immediately ready: 'What, then, should be done with and for children in this sphere?', and one is at a loss for an answer. In this, however, one is not alone. Whenever a society officially decides that it is not a Christian society, as, for example, in the case of France, or when it approaches that position, there must inevitably be an agonizing struggle to discover whether there is an agreed basis for the moral and religious training of the young, and what it may be, since society by its nature cannot remain morally neutral in all things. Since, however, this kind of struggle is already going on in society with regard to its adults, as may be seen from the present discussion of humanism, it can only be a matter of time before it has to be faced with regard to children, if the present situation is not to continue whereby parents pass the buck to the school to instruct their children in the rudiments of a faith in which they themselves do not believe or participate, or if the whole operation is not done with the tongue in the cheek.

The following tentative suggestions may be made, though out of great ignorance. It would seem that what the very young child is at is exploring the world as it finds it, generally tactually. Here 'love pussy' means to stroke, feel or hug pussy. From this proceeds an expanding exploration of things in which wonder and surprise march along with a growing factual knowledge and description of how things are or appear to be. A lot of lies have to be told through over-simplification, but they are of the kind whose correction later on does not cause much trouble, since the correction can generally be made to cohere with the original explanation. At this stage it is not inconsistent to teach God as creator, as it seems natural for the child that this should be so, and invariably leads to the question of who made God. This is succeeded by a stage in which greater attention is paid to persons and their actions, generally of a heroic kind and accompanied by a good deal of moral approval or disapproval, which also can lead to its own falsities of good kings and bad kings. Here some use could be made of the Bible, and especially of the Old Testament, not because it is the Bible, but because the Bible offers some particularly good examples forcefully told – though even this will generally be against the trend of the Bible itself, which, because of its strong theological concentration, hardly ever thinks or speaks in terms of the heroic. But it is the further adolescent and reflective stages that are crucial, and when the damage is done. In discussions of this subject it is often the earlier stages which are chiefly in mind, but it does not matter all that much what happens at the conscious level at these stages (it matters very much what happens at the subconscious level), and if scriptural knowledge, along with a lot else, falls away. But at the conscious level at the adolescent stage it matters a great deal what is taken on into the foundations of the adult life. Where the young are let down at this stage is not in the absence of scripture or divinity in the generally accepted sense, but rather in its presence, and in the absence of an adequate introduction to philosophy and philosophical thinking, using those terms in a broad sense. The questions which are naturally raised at this stage – or which ought to be evoked, if education and the life of society are not such as to cause them to be raised naturally and before the young begin to be swallowed up in the business of earning a living – are primarily philosophical questions. They are questions about coherence and meaning, either in the physical sphere (as for example about the relation between the evolutionary picture of man and any other picture), or in the moral sphere (as for example about the problem of evil – not for nothing does 'protest' begin here). It is a let-down at the most sensitive point if and when such questions are met with more scriptural information, since scripture at best is only very indirectly concerned with them, and can only appear as dogmatic and arbitrary when used to answer them. The gospel of Christ, from its basis of a long formulated belief in God and of his moral law, passes by many of these questions, which are nevertheless questions which have to be asked. It is also a let-down if what is offered at this juncture is a course in the comparative study of religions. Not that this should not be taught. The teaching of Christianity will in the future increasingly take place alongside the comparative study of religions, and ought to do so, if only for the reason that the record of Christianity in taking account of the existence of other religions has been a poor one from the start. But it will not do at this juncture, because it is not an answer to the questions which are actually being asked, and may therefore become a diversionary manoeuvre to dodge them. It does not present the young with a real and viable option, and no one will as a result of it buy a prayer mat and orient his prayers towards Mecca. There is only one live option at the moment, which is to be a humanist or a humanist; to believe in and live by some collection of ideas of what man is and is meant to be, if one is able to believe it possible to speak about 'man' as such. It is the absence of a sufficient supply of men and women at their elbows capable not of providing answers but of guiding the discussion of the questions which leads to the greatest hiatus in the spiritual development of children at its most sensitive point. Another and rather old-fashioned way of saying the same thing would be that our greatest gap is the lack of a natural theology, which is perhaps the only kind of theology one ought to have between the ages of sixteen and nineteen. But the circumstances are that we do not now have it, and that scripture is not designed to supply it. But the fact and the consequences of not having it ought not to be masked, and in its absence we ought to be more prepared than we are to grapple with the situation of not having it, and to agonize over the questions to which natural theology, when it exists, thinks it has the answers. To try to make scripture provide answers here is to try to make it do what it cannot, just as some theologians in throwing over the idea of God have attempted to make the word 'Jesus' do all the work which the word 'God' once did. For scripture, or at least the New Testament, begins further on than this, where the supposed answers of natural theology or its lack of answers reveal something of the barrenness of the land. This is part of what I have referred to as the missionary situation, namely a church on the one hand which, in a desperate attempt to hold on to what it thought it had, becomes more and more child-centred, and therefore unable to appreciate the essentially adult nature of its gospel; and on the other hand an increasing number of the young who grow into maturity immunized against the gospel because they have been through a process in which the New Testament has been so adapted to their imagined needs that their abiding impression is of having grown out of it and of having seen through it. And at a time when one of the characteristics of the young is a determination not to be taken in, this is a very serious matter.

NOTES

1. See E. Käsemann, 'Thoughts on the Present Controversy about Scriptural Interpretation', *New Testament Questions of Today*, Eng. trans., SCM Press 1969, pp. 268ff.
2. C. H. Dodd, *The Interpretation of the Fourth Gospel,* Cambridge University Press 1953.

4

Is 'the Jesus of History' Important?

It would be easy to keep this question well within academic boundaries, as it has a strong academic side, and belongs with a current phase of technical gospel analysis which goes under the title of 'the new quest of the historical Jesus'. The old quest was that documented by Albert Schweitzer in his book *Von Reimarus zu Wrede*, which had for its title in the English translation *The Quest of the Historical Jesus*,[1] and which surveyed the lives of Jesus written in the nineteenth century under the impulse of the critical analysis of the gospels as then understood and practised. Since then a great deal of further analysis of the gospels has taken place, much of it associated with the form-critical method, and with the generally sceptical conclusions about the historicity of the events and sayings in the sources at which its practitioners, especially Rudolf Bultmann, are held to arrive (though when one reads his books his conclusions are often found to be less sceptical than alleged). The new quest was initiated, significantly – for it exhibits something of the ethos and methods of biblical criticism – not by his opponents but by his most able pupils, Bornkamm, Ebeling, Fuchs, Käsemann. These have put a question mark against an almost complete disjunction between what Jesus was considered to have done and said on the one hand and the kerygma or proclamation about him as a saving message on the other. They have attempted to come at this by laying down ever more exact criteria for distinguishing between what Jesus said and what in the gospels can be put down to (*a*) contemporary Judaism, or (*b*) the faith of the primitive church, and so hope to get at the authentic sayings and the authentic form of such sayings by this route. The criteria are not foolproof. If Jesus had ever happened to echo an opinion of contemporary Judaism he could not be known to have done so by this test, and our knowledge of the faith of the primitive church is too fragmentary to be sure that we could always recognize it when we saw it. These scholars also operate with a somewhat more flexible conception of history, in which a man's behaviour as well as his words are taken as indications of his purpose; much emphasis is laid, for example, on Jesus' consorting with publicans and sinners as evidence of his purpose. This new quest has been responsible for a spate of writing in book, pamphlet and article, of which a useful review and discussion in English is F. G. Downing's *The Church and Jesus*.[2] One could then run for cover by attempting some kind of survey of this literature, and perhaps offer one's own view in face of the fluctuating position of the betting. For in all academic disciplines there is at some point an element of 'a game' involved, as the philosophers are prepared to acknowledge when they speak of 'playing language games', and this element does not disappear just because the subject is serious. But supposing such a survey could be made in any space short of a book, would it be of much assistance to anyone? Those who repudiate any significance in gospel criticism on the ground that faith cannot be made dependent on historical research would be in a strong position here; it certainly cannot depend on the latest reports on how much or how little this or that scholar is allowing by way of historicity. But there is a level at which faith is affected by historical research on this question, and at the risk of dealing only in vague generalizations one may come at it as a practical question which could affect us all.

The phrase 'the Jesus of history', or some such term, is an unusual one. Our forefathers before the nineteenth century would not have recognized nor understood it. If one speaks of 'the Napoleon of history' one means to distinguish between the Napoleon who emerges from a critical examination of the available sources and the figure who became, perhaps to some extent in his lifetime, surrounded by legend. But the Christian church knew no such distinction. For the greater part of its life, so far as the available sources, the gospels, were concerned, it has lived by harmonies. There were known to be inconsistencies, even contradictions here, but they were not formulated as problems, nor made the starting point of analysis. Somehow, and often with great ingenuity, the four accounts were fitted into a single story or mosaic. In this single story all individual stories were on all fours with one another. No problem arose in the mind concerning any possible influence upon the narrative of Jesus of Nazareth of faith in Christ the Lord, and no distinction was made so far as historical happening was concerned between the birth of Jesus, his Galilean healing and teaching, his transfiguration, his parables, his death and resurrection. All were historical and theological at the same time. There was a complete continuity between Jesus preaching and the Jesus preached, and for those who can hold to this there is still no problem. How, then, did a change of attitude ever arise? This is connected with the birth of the modern study of history in general. Like all great changes in human attitudes it is somewhat mysterious and complex, and one is not sure of being able to account for it completely. But so far from it being the case, as is often supposed, that the attitudes and techniques which now belong to what we call the modern study of history were first perfected in the history faculties and were then applied reluctantly to biblical studies, almost the opposite is the case. Much of what we mean by the modern study of history saw its beginnings in the theological faculties, as the theologians were led to fashion and sharpen the tools they needed for work upon what turned out to be one of, if not the most complex historical problems, that presented by the gospel narratives of Jesus.

The change had something to do with an alteration of attitude towards the sources, from one which was basically receptive of what was contained in them to one which was basically suspicious. This took place first in relation to the Bible, because already in the seventeenth and eighteenth centuries a conflict had arisen between the Bible and science in respect of space (Galileo), of time (the question of the age of the world), and of geography (the discovery of Australia created a shock because it could not be fitted into the lands referred to in the Bible). The result was the possibility of a cleavage between fact and statements of faith in the highest authority then known. Only later was this attitude applied to history, so as to transform it from the writing of annals or chronicles to what we now mean by it. In 1796-7 Gottfried Herder, who had previously undermined the authority of Homer by maintaining that the Homeric poems were the work of a number of individual rhapsodists, published works in which he propounded two theses – that the Fourth Gospel must be kept separate from the synoptic gospels and evaluated separately, and, anticipating form-criticism by a century and a half, that the material of the synoptic gospels was, as it were, the product of rhapsodists, who had handed on independent oral units of tradition without biographical interest.[3] There is something very modern in the sound of these two theses, and they are still clearly recognizable as the thin end of the wedge of what we know as critical and historical analysis of the gospels. Once inserted the wedge could be driven in deeper and deeper. This was done first by literary analysis – the synoptic problem and what went with it – which dealt a death blow to harmonization, since what appeared in one gospel could be shown to have been taken from another and modified in the process, and what was responsible for the modification was the writer's own faith and understanding. Thus, to cite a simple example, if it could be shown that in writing the words 'If any man would come after me let him deny himself and take up his cross daily and follow me' Luke had copied them from Mark, and that in so copying he had added the word 'daily', and that by his addition he had significantly modified the meaning of the saying, then one was face to face not with two things which had somehow to be harmonized, but with a traceable stage in the transmission of a tradition, in which the end result was due to an interaction between something said and how that something had been later applied, and the later application had now been taken up into the gospel tradition itself. The wedge was driven in further by form-criticism, which in asking how the units of the gospel material came to be in the shape they were was also asking questions about the needs and motive forces in the early Christian communities which had caused this or that to be handed down in this or that form, so that both the needs and their satisfaction became part of the tradition itself. There was and is, of course, ample room for very subjective judgments and for all kind of error in this. Nevertheless, the historian of Christian origins, along with the preacher in the pulpit, have become aware in this way of the interpretative element which may belong to any fragment of the tradition, and of this element having its source in a post-Easter faith which was different in standpoint from a pre-Easter situation, however organically connected with it.

This last point, however, only draws attention to a feature of the

New Testament which has been there all along. Analytical study of this kind, full of mistakes as it may be, does not do violence to the material by forcing it into a mould for which it was never meant, but does something to bring to light its nature. For what makes the historical problem for Christianity so complex is that the New Testament has always been made up of two kinds of writings, those which narrate the events and sayings out of which Christianity is supposed to have arisen, and those which came out of the Christianity which did arise, and the connection between the two is hardly ever obvious and clear. The contents of the second type do not consist of a repetition of the contents of the first type, nor do the contents of the first type consist of a blueprint for the contents of the second. One may suspect that there may have been an interaction between them, though we are seldom in a position to put a finger on it. When we are, the consequences can be far-reaching. Thus the Fourth Gospel appears to be closely related to that person or school of thought from which the Johannine Epistles proceeded, so that whatever historical traditions have gone to this gospel's composition, one element has certainly gone into it, viz. that the Christ of the Fourth Gospel talks the language and theology of these epistles. Thus there is always a possibility that an interaction between words and events and the use they have been put to has to be considered, and in some cases it is a necessity for making sense of a passage. In the resurrection narratives, for example, the force of the event is conveyed less by the account of the appearances themselves than by the words spoken by the risen Lord, and these are spoken in Matthean, Lucan or Johannine accents respectively according to the gospel concerned. But this could also apply to parables.

Are we landed with this for good? It is unwise to dogmatize about the future; many unexpected things happen. One possible reaction is to sit under one's umbrella in hope that the rain will stop. One might say that biblical criticism has been going through a perverse phase, and that if one waits long enough the wheel will come full circle, and all will be traditional again. But this is very doubtful. There are some things which come to stay. Just as something like a concept of evolution is likely to be a permanent accompaniment of human thinking however else we may come to look at man, so it is likely that something like the historical method – though not necessarily in its present form, and probably not with its present results – will be a permanent feature in human thinking about the past and about its documents, and therefore about Christianity in so far as it is bound to its past and its documents. We cannot simply wish this away or wait till the tyranny is overpast. We have to learn to live with it, and this is something different in prospect from knowing the latest state of the game in the quest of the historical Jesus. What are its consequences?

One does not see one's way clearly in this and can only think and talk around it. 'Is the Jesus of History Important?' is an easier form of the question, since it invites an answer 'Yes' or 'No'. There have occasionally been those who have answered 'No', notably the Roman Catholic modernists in the early years of this century who, alas, were cut off by excommunication before they were allowed to have their full say, or their position could run the full gauntlet of criticism. Their rejoinder to the German liberals and to the quest of the historical Jesus as it then stood was that Christianity does not live by faithfulness to a Jesus of history, but by the worship of the Son of God. It is a cult; if you like, the supreme mystery religion of all time, which by its doctrine and sacraments produces saints. No doubt they were too sweeping, and the philosophy through which they said what they had to say would not stand up to scrutiny now; but it is perhaps a pity that they were not allowed to have their full say, as they faced biblical theology with questions it has tended to by-pass rather than to answer, particularly the extent to which Christianity is a mystery cult, and why it did not go the way of the other cults. And even now they raise the question whether room is to be found in the church for those whose answer to the question 'Is the Jesus of history important?' would be 'No'. Or there is the approach from the Protestant side of the book which, though written in 1892, has only recently been translated into English and has only recently begun to exercise influence – Martin Kähler's *The So-Called Historical Jesus and the Historical Biblical Christ*.[4] For Kähler the gospels are confessional and proclamatory; they preclude a life of Jesus, and the idea is ridiculous that faith can rest upon research or upon a scientifically reconstructed historical basis. The only historical Jesus there is, that is, the only Jesus who operates in history, is the preached Christ of the apostles. This is the only Jesus there is to be met.

These cuttings of the Gordian knot remain unsatisfactory to many, and the answer to the question would generally continue to be 'Yes'. But in that case the question can be posed in forms which make it more difficult to answer, such as 'How is the Jesus of history important?', or 'How important is the Jesus of history?' How many beans make five? How many historical facts, in an unsophisticated meaning of the word 'historical', go to make a gospel, and of what kind do they have to be? This way of putting the question may sound frivolous, but it is not so in face of a curious feature of some of the theological writing of our time, which combines an emphatic insistence in general on the historical element as the hallmark of Christianity as a religion with an uncertainty about the historical authenticity of any one event in it in particular. Are there guidelines here?

We start from Christianity itself. Whether as individuals or as members of a community, or simply as living in the twentieth century, we do not start with immediate contact with a Jesus of history, or even with the 'word of God', but with Christianity as something which has persisted to the present time, and is simply there. This has its own problems, which have become more acute. What is Christianity in its essence, and how does one reform it according to its essence? For the Reformers this was easier. The rot had set in just outside the New Testament and the New Testament was itself the instrument of reform, though Luther had some disturbing thoughts about first and second grade writings within the New Testament itself which were not taken up. Some would now think the rot had set in within the New Testament itself according to their prior judgment of where the essence lies. But leaving these problems aside, we start from Christianity, and Christianity is a form of salvation or of saving truth. It proclaims the possibility of a union with God and his will, of an alignment of human life with creation and the intention of the creator, of a community of mankind in essentials, of deliverance from the frustration caused by time and its passing or by evil and its enslaving into freedom and loving and purposeful action. It promises the ultimate mastery of all that spells death, and the possibility of new beginnings and new life within the apparently fate-determined, behaviouristic, cause-and-effect, space-time existence.

How far is all this connected with Jesus and not simply with

God? How far does the statement 'God is love', in order to be true and effective, have to be shown to have an organic connection with what Jesus said and did? We may say that empirically it has had that connection in the community of life which constitutes the church, stretching from its beginning to the present time. But this does not carry us very far unless one adopts Kähler's position that the only historical Jesus is the preached Jesus. For the difficulty here, even from the position of the New Testament itself, is that the statements about Jesus within the New Testament and beyond it which have supported the truth that God is love, or that Christianity is saving truth proclaiming the possibility of union with God and his will, and so on, have not been statements of a historical kind about him but of a theological kind – that he is Messiah, Son of man, Son of God, etc. Some would say of a 'mythological' kind, meaning by 'mythological', statements about divine action in the world, even about divine transaction. If one says 'Jesus is Lord', or spells this out with the hymn in Philippians 2 by saying that 'being in the form of God ... he poured himself out and took upon himself the form of a servant ... and was obedient to death, even the death of the cross', or says 'God so loved the world that he gave his only begotten Son ...', the historical element is reduced in the first case to the name 'Jesus', in the second to 'the death of the cross', and in the third hardly appears at all. The effective force of these statements lies in their being statements about the divine dealing with the world, with its possibilities, problems and frustrations, and they are chiefly statements about suffering, death and resurrection, or in the case of the Fourth Gospel about divine visitation. This is to speak very like the mystery cults or Gnosticism, and the question of the relation between Christianity and the mystery cults and Gnosticism has been perhaps too easily dealt with in the past, sometimes because the question has been put too crudely. But in some measure the present problem of the historical Jesus is the problem of Gnosticism over again in a new form, posed not in the metaphysical terms of matter and spirit but in terms of the historical and the non-historical and of the relation between them.

Along these lines the empirical question may be posed why Christianity did not go the way of the other cults and slowly evaporate. Could this be because of the historical element in it? A cult of salvation or a gnosis tend to be deifications of some aspect of existence, generally the aspects of life and death, or to be a deliverance out of life in its temporal and temporary form. Christian salvation, however, has about it a strong element of the consummation of this world. This relates to the Jewish background upon which it emerged. Jewish salvation is closely connected with history; too closely, indeed, since in its simplest form it can be identified with a divinely overruled history of Israel in an ideal kingdom governed by an ideal David. Christianity had to break with this, to go to the world, and to make contact with what was not Jewish. One of the ways in which the riddle of New Testament Christianity presents itself is in the juxtaposition, especially in Paul and John, of what is Jewish with what is non-Jewish. The defect of the doctrine of 'salvation history' as presented in the writings of Oscar Cullmann is that it presupposes a kind of canal of sacred event or divine action flowing within the bounds of the world's history, with the consequent doubtful definitions and demarcations which go with determining where the canal is to be found. Nevertheless, Christianity brings along with it certain permanent Jewish elements which differentiate it from the general pattern of salvation cult. One example may be given from its central point, that of the resurrection. Christianity avoids being a cult of a dying and living (or, coming-to-life-again) Lord, which is a deification of the pattern of nature, since Jesus is not, except occasionally in the Fourth Gospel, the author of his own life beyond death. Its author is the transcendent creator acting towards his creation in the person of Jesus. Since faith in the resurrection of Jesus is the standpoint from which all the New Testament writings, including the gospels, are written, the theocentric character of the gospel is thereby established. It is not a cult of Jesus. There is no transcendent creator behind Mithra or Isis; they are lords in their own right. But behind Jesus is the transcendent creator, and resurrection is his supreme creative action towards the creation and human existence. Resurrection is not a delivery of Jesus out of the world, but the investing of his human existence with authority and power. For this to be so, there must be both the transcendent creator and also as the object of his action someone who has a truly human existence. It cannot concern God and a symbol, or noun or *x*; otherwise Christianity loses its character in respect of this world.

But then the question is 'How much history?' Will it do to have enough to be able to say that Jesus was human and historical, but not enough to be able to go into any significant detail as to the shape of that humanity or historical existence, as with the Creed, when it leaps from 'born of the Virgin Mary' to 'suffered under Pontius Pilate'? If it is essential for Christianity as saving truth to be able to say that the Christ who is also was, is it sufficient to be able simply to say that he was, or must we be able to say of what that 'wasness' was made up? Here we are back again not particularly with critical analysis, but simply with the New Testament itself, for there his 'isness' was not necessarily conveyed by a repetition of his 'wasness'. To apprehend the truth of being 'in Christ' or that one was justified by faith one did not, apparently, have to know that a historical Jesus called fishermen or associated with outcasts.

This raises from another angle the vexed question of the origin and purpose of the gospels. They are not the earliest books in the New Testament, and the Christian communities had got on without them, though presumably not without some of the material of which they came to be composed, even if this material was not in the form of a historical sequence. Why were they written? The answers given in the text-books – that the original (apostolic?) eye-witnesses were dying off, and that the expectation of the end was fading – are not particularly convincing. The answer is perhaps different in the case of each gospel. But it has been suggested (e.g. by Käsemann[5]) that each in its own way was an attempt to anchor spiritual experience to the acts and words of Jesus in protest against that experience going its own way unchecked, and producing results which someone felt instinctively to be erroneous. Of such a spirituality we probably have an instance in the church in Corinth, and in I Corinthians an attempt to deal with those who thought that they were already in the kingdom of God and beyond resurrection. Paul does not deal with this by appeal to a historical Jesus but by reference to the death of Christ. The resurrection is the exaltation of the humble and rejected one, and the Christian life is therefore not the fully resurrected life but a *via crucis* in the light of a coming resurrection. It could be that the gospels had a similar purpose, and that their material was not simply a reflection of a post-Easter spirituality but a check on it.

Thus the Fourth Gospel comes from the same sphere of thought as I John, where there is a bitter conflict over the 'spirits', which are to be tested, and the test is over the ability to say that the Christ has come in the flesh. So in the Fourth Gospel it is insisted that the Word became flesh and that the Spirit does not have an independent mission of his own, but is to take the words of Jesus and expound them to the disciples. But the complexity of the problem then appears with the consideration that perhaps none of the words of Jesus in this gospel is historical, i.e. was spoken as it is now written. It is also possible that Matthew's Gospel is what it is in its selection of material, shape, and emphasis because it is designed to oppose, that is, to deny the true spirituality of, those who by-passed or questioned the permanent validity of the Jewish Law in the proclamation of the gospel to the Gentiles. And one may ask whether in doing this it has made Jesus the spokesman of a Jewish Christianity. Contrariwise, Mark's Gospel has been expounded by at least one scholar (E. Trocmé[6]) as being intended by its selection of material, shape and emphasis to be a protest against a slackening of the Gentile mission as a result of the influence of the Jerusalem church. If something like this is the case, then the very production of the gospels may have followed the order not of starting with cause and proceeding to effect, but of starting with effect in the form of the spirituality with which the evangelist was cognizant, and of providing it with a basis in the words and acts of Jesus as those had come down to him as a means of propagating that spirituality. Only in Luke-Acts, as the one instance of a gospel with a sequel, are cause and effect presented in that order; but since it is without doubt that one of the main motives for the writing of Luke-Acts was to present Christianity to the outside world as a movement which carried all before it despite opposition, and as innocent of offence so far as the state was concerned, the shape and emphasis of the first volume may have been considerably influenced by the shape which the second was to take.

Only if the gospels are the result of arguing back from effect to cause can it be explained why the passion and resurrection narratives are so very different in them. Clearly the passion and resurrection narratives dominate in the gospels because the passion and resurrection of Christ were known to be the core of Christian spirituality. But what the death and resurrection mean, and how they are to be understood, varied a great deal to judge from the differences in the narratives. So much are these religious narratives, expressing theological viewpoints, that it is difficult to gather from them the facts of the situation. Thus they contribute next to no certain evidence upon a matter on which the whole story hangs, and which would influence any estimate of the motives of the persons concerned, namely, whether the Jewish Sanhedrin did or did not have the right of administering the capital penalty. So also they do not provide the means for discerning clearly how the particular antagonisms of the Galilean ministry were connected with the antagonisms in Jerusalem; in other words for answering that part of the question 'How important is the Jesus of history?' which consists in the question 'How – historically – did Jesus come to be put to death?'

In the end, however, the question comes to a head over the ministry of word and work, and in an acute form. The gospel in the epistles does not refer to this ministry. There it is God's gospel, and is concerned with God's action towards Israel and so towards men through the crucified and risen Messiah. It is eschatological; that is, a final and ultimate address to and communication with men, and this is expressed by terms like Messiah and Lord. The question then is whether, and in what way, a historical Jesus spoke and acted so as to give rise to this, or whether this was something which got going, we know not how, from an outburst of religious energy which we call Easter and Pentecost, and which was then somehow fathered on Jesus. In the end this may come down to a critical assessment of what Jesus meant by the term 'the kingdom of God', of which statements about it can with probability be assigned to him, and of how his healing work, parables and sayings were related to it. For, on the evidence of the gospels themselves, it is very doubtful whether he thought of himself as the Messiah. But the kingdom of God is also an eschatological term, and in the way in which it is used in the gospels it does not simply designate a future consummation by God of his work, but also points to the quality and meaning of Jesus' historical actions and the response they demand. To this extent it would not only be the preached gospel in which the salvation of God and the present time and life of men were brought together on the basis that Jesus, and not some x, is the Messiah; but the proclamation of this union of the future and the present, and of God with man, would have been made somewhere, sometime, within the circumstances of a (Jewish) human life. And since human beings belong somewhere and to some time, and live in human circumstances, it may be held that the Jesus of history is important. But this is not a matter only of academic study. When one is asked to pronounce from an academic angle on Schonfield's *The Passover Plot*,[7] or Pasolini's *The Gospel according to St Matthew*, or Dennis Potter's *The Son of Man*, which represent more public presentations of the problem of the historical Jesus, what is one to say? The only answers one feels able honestly to give are that, in the first place, the dramatist has a free rein and his play must be judged by standards of dramatic integrity, but that in the second place the only theological and critical criterion which can be applied is whether the Christ depicted is or is not the kind of figure from which Christianity could be supposed to have emerged, at whatever remove or stage of subsequent development. The question remains whether this is enough, and whether we have to come to terms with this being enough. Or to put it another way, are there to be legitimately within the church different kinds of Christian faith, in which different sorts of historical elements have differing amounts of importance at different points, varying from very great importance indeed to practically no importance at all?

NOTES

1. A. Schweitzer, *The Quest of the Historical Jesus*, Eng. trans., A. and C. Black 1910; 3rd ed. with new introduction, 1954.

2. F. G. Downing, *The Church and Jesus* (Studies in Biblical Theology, Second Series 10), SCM Press 1968.

3. J. G. Herder, *Vom Erlöser der Menschen*, 1796; *Von Gottes Sohn, der Welt Heiland*, 1797.

4. M. Kähler, *The So-Called Historical Jesus and the Historical, Biblical Christ*, Eng. trans. by C. E. Braaten, Fortress Press, Philadelphia 1964.

5. E. Käsemann, 'Blind Alleys in the "Jesus of History" Controversy', *New Testament Questions of Today*, 1969, pp.62ff.

6. E. Trocmé, *La formation de l'Évangile selon Marc* (Études d'histoire et de philosophie religieuses 57), Presses universitaires 1963, pp.104ff, 195ff.

7. H. J. Schonfield, *The Passover Plot*, Hutchinson 1965.

5

Resurrection in the New Testament and Now

A reviewer of a book which I had written recently on *Resurrection and the New Testament*[1] complained that it was not the study in biblical theology to be expected since it was too preoccupied with the literary and historical questions involved to say anything which could be directed towards the materialism and purposelessness of the present times. Though this was not the scope and intention of the book, and New Testament subjects are to be studied in their own right and their own terms, the criticism is not without justification and is to be taken to heart. As with questions like the quest of the historical Jesus, so here, it is always possible to play for safety by keeping within the confines of academic discipline and discussion. It has been the nemesis of the biblical theology of the last few decades that it has unduly restricted theological thinking within the terminology and thought-forms of the Bible itself. This has gone along with a renewed insistence on the New Testament as holy and apostolic book. Whatever status, however, we may assign to the New Testament writings, they cannot be less than guide-posts towards a continuation of that exploration of human life with the aid of Christian faith and hope that has already begun within them, or than raw material for that exploration however difficult it may turn out to be. And in the case of 'resurrection' it proves to be very difficult indeed.

The contents of the three chapters in the book referred to above were roughly as follows. Firstly, though resurrection is clearly central to the New Testament message, the concept was a latecomer in Judaism, appearing for certain only in one passage in the Old Testament and developing only in the period between the Old and New Testaments. The development took three forms. There was firstly that found in II Maccabees, where resurrection appears along with a doctrine of martyrdom, and it is the expectation of the martyrs that through their faithfulness to death they would be resurrected to this earth to partake of the kingdom of God for which they had suffered. There was secondly that taken in apocalyptic works under the influence of the originally Zoroastrian idea that there was to be a universal moral judgment, in which resurrection was simply one feature in a programme, the feature which enabled the dead to be brought to the judgment in a recognizable bodily form. And there was thirdly that also found in apocalyptic works, but mainly in wisdom books such as the Wisdom of Solomon and IV Maccabees, where it is a hybrid with the Greek doctrine of immortality, and is more concerned with survival from death and temporality, though it is never the pure philosophical doctrine, since eternal life is not the inalienable possession of man but is the gift of God to the deserving. A question-mark may therefore be placed against the view that by the first century AD resurrection was part of a Jewish orthodoxy, and wide variations in thought about it as to the persons, time, place and mode involved might indicate that it was still very much a matter of speculation. The most recent background evidence, that supplied by the Qumran scrolls, might support this, since in the scrolls so far available there is no undisputed evidence for a belief in resurrection. Its centrality in the New Testament may have to be sought within the event itself rather than in the Jewish background.

Secondly, in examining the resurrection tradition itself, chiefly I Corinthians 15 and the resurrection narratives in the gospels, it was contended that though the tradition was not single, uniform or stereotyped, but rather multiple, varied and with a wide spread, it was out of the question to harmonize these traditions, as they did not turn out to be pieces in a jig-saw, which could be fitted together albeit with some gaps, but rather each was itself a self-contained whole differing to a considerable degree from other self-contained wholes. Not only did the early formula in I Corinthians 15 have little if anything to reflect it in the gospel narratives and *vice versa*, but within the gospel traditions themselves there are wide variations in theology corresponding to the different theologies of the individual gospels in which those narratives are found as their climax. In the gospel narratives the meaning of the resurrection is conveyed primarily through the words which the risen Lord utters, and these words are not only variant, but are plainly those of a Matthean, Lucan and Johannine Lord respectively. Thus despite the multiple tradition it is, in fact, very difficult to penetrate to what the resurrection itself may have been, and this is largely due to the incorporation into it of what came to be apprehended through the resurrection faith – the exaltation of Jesus as Lord, the gift of the Spirit and the apostolic mission to the world.

Thirdly, this resurrection faith was explored in the New Testament literature, and especially in Paul. From a fairly simple re-active understanding, in which resurrection is God's reversal of what men had done in the crucifixion, it is brought into connection with all the major points in the gospel. As interchangeable with the concept of exaltation, and as a synonym for it, it is the basis of the lordship, first over the church and then over the universe, of the man Jesus. This is first asserted in relation to the parousia, which is expected as the necessary and imminent completion of his work and career. Hence the first problem to be faced was that of Christians who had died before it and of how they stood with respect to the corporate transformation of all believers, and perhaps of the universe, which was to accompany the final manifestation of their and its Lord. But alongside with, and perhaps gradually replacing this attention to the future manifestation, there came to be a stress on the measure of resurrection, of new and eternal life, which was already experienced by the believers, so that resurrection becomes both a future and a present thing, and is brought into closer connection with the Christian life. Thus Paul can bring it into connection with justification when he says that Christ was raised for our justification, and it is already experienced by the apostle within, and not as a reversal of, his present sufferings. It brings the Spirit, who is not only an earnest of a future glory but a present foretaste of it. In I Peter it is that which brings about a rebirth now as well as pointing to an incorruptible future salvation, and in the Johannine writings it is, in the form of eternal life, a present possession of the believer, and a future resurrection has moved from the centre to the circumference.

Assuming that all this is not a gross distortion of the matter so far as the New Testament is concerned, what may it be said to provide by way of informing the mind in its exploration of human life with Christian faith and hope? Two preliminary observations may be made. The first is that there is no direct carry over from the New Testament to the present at certain vital points. Our chief concern with the matter will be with the resurrection of believers, as it came to be in the second and third centuries, when it was at the centre of theological debate. But in the New Testament it is the resurrection of Christ which is at the centre, and it is not evident how the one is related to the other. Thus in the *locus classicus*, I Corinthians 15, Paul can argue on the basis of the resurrection of Christ that the believer will wear the image of the heavenly man, but in expounding the nature of the resurrection or spiritual 'body' he does not appear to be reading it off as a conclusion from the risen 'body' of Christ. When a New Testament writer undertakes to fill out what it means to be risen with Christ he generally speaks not in terms of resurrection but of 'exaltation' or glory. He is not thinking, and nor shall we, in terms of empty tombs, of passing through closed doors, of travelling along roads or of eating fish, which is how the gospel narratives came to depict the risen Christ. This draws attention to the fact that in the New Testament the resurrection in some respects is peculiar to Christ, and that it functions for him as a special case from which general conclusions cannot be drawn. And even in his case it functions in a special way, in being resurrection to a temporary state with the limited purpose of conveying to the disciples his full status. Once that is done he appears as the risen one no longer, and it is only in his exalted or glorified state that parallels can be drawn between him and the believer. Thus there are limitations at the outset to the extent that resurrection, in the form of the resurrection of Christ, is informative.

The second preliminary observation concerns language, though it is not simply concerned with language, since language clothes thought. The point may be put for convenience through the contrary positions held by two German writers on the subject, Willi Marxsen and Wolfhart Pannenberg. Marxsen contends, surely rightly, that the word 'resurrection' and the concept arose within the apocalyptic thought which developed in Judaism. It is not a neutral word for a description of an event, but an interpretative word, which by its use from the beginning imparted to the event, whatever it was, a particular meaning governed by Jewish apocalyptic and anthropological thought-forms. He would therefore wish to distinguish the essence of the Easter faith as the permanent presence of Jesus as the living one from 'resurrection' as a mode of conceptualizing this, which, as conditioned by a first-century apocalyptic, we cannot share.[2] Pannenberg, on the other hand, sees the resurrection as absolutely central to, because a paradigm of, an understanding of Christianity which overcomes the hiatus between fact and interpretation, event and faith, by identifying theology and history. The whole of reality is history, and this can be so because history only comes to us within a tradition in which there are no bare facts. History always brings its meaning along with it, this meaning being involved in its future. The resurrection of Jesus – the coming to life again of a man by the action of God in such a way that he lives for ever – can only be apprehended as divine revelation in terms of the expected universal resurrection of the dead which belonged to that tradition in the light of which Jesus lived and taught. Thus Pannenberg insists that resurrection is not to be separated from these apocalyptic categories (the last judgment, the general resurrection, the parousia etc.); they remain valid and may not be exchanged for any others. So while resurrection is a metaphor (he identifies it with waking from sleep) it is what he calls an absolute metaphor, and is not replaceable.[3]

This can become a very practical and urgent question, as, for instance, in attempting to revise in a Liturgical Commission the service for the Burial of the Dead, when the validity and advisability of New Testament language have to be considered. And it would seem that the language, for example, of sleep is not irreplaceable metaphor, but is metaphor which, even if it is used at all, should never be pressed. It seems to have been from very early times and in many cultures simply a metaphor for the dead, and cannot be held to supply reliable information about the dead. It is used in this conventional way in the New Testament, and in the few indirect and elusive references which Paul makes to his dying before the parousia he does not seem to contemplate it as a sleeping existence, but as being with Christ, whatever that may mean. If Marxsen's position is accepted, then it is immediately drawn into the wider programme of 'demythologizing' New Testament language and its attendant difficulties. The cry is wholly justified that if the modern man rejects the gospel, let it be the gospel he rejects and not something to which he cannot commit himself because, with the best will in the world, he cannot think like a first-century Jew. But this leaves unsolved two problems. The first is how we are to know that we have first comprehended what is to be translated into modern terms if it has already been defined as that which we cannot ourselves think; and the second is how we are to know whether in the translation we have rendered all that needs to be rendered of the original and have not dropped out something in the process. For it may be that in hearing the gospel the modern man may have to listen to some things which contradict his normal way of thinking, and this might be so particularly in relation to resurrection.

With these preliminary observations in mind the following points may be tentatively advanced. Firstly, the resurrection language of the New Testament is pre-eminently God language. That must be said, whatever acute difficulties it brings with it in view of our present embarrassment about God language. For it is in being God language that its force lies. This can be seen quite clearly. The subject of the verb 'to raise' is always God, or the verbs are used in the passive, which in Semitic idiom is one way of conveying God as the subject (the only exception is the Fourth Gospel, and then only in part). In fact, 'he who raised Jesus from the dead' has become in parts of the New Testament a mode of describing God in his being God. It was resurrection language which prevented Christianity from becoming a cult of the Lord Jesus. The matter is, indeed, nicely balanced, for whereas according to Paul, perhaps here quoting tradition, it is precisely the resurrection which makes possible the confession 'Jesus is Lord', it is also the resurrection which forbids the statement becoming the watchword of a Jesus cult. The language is thus God language, and if this has to be given up as impossible no amount of 'Jesus language' will do what is done in the New Testament through the relation and interaction between Jesus and God.

But, more precisely, resurrection poses the question not only of the possibility and validity of God language in general, but of language about divine creation in particular. This was already so within the original apocalyptic schema itself, which apparently operated on the principle that the *Endzeit* reproduces the *Urzeit*, the end is a return to the beginning, though now by way of the conditions which have pertained in between as the result of creation. This appears in the New Testament also, when resurrection is brought into connection with what is called 'new creation'. The question which then has to be asked is whether we are capable of using the word creation with full seriousness, or only as a loose term to impart a kind of flavour to what exists. Creation means that what exists exists as a whole, and as the result of a will and action outside anything it is itself capable of, and – if it is theistic and not deistic creation – that this will is involved with, is committed to, and is present with, that which it has caused to exist. From this angle resurrection is no less and no more than the working through of the concept of creation to its end. It is noteworthy that the apologists and fathers of the second century, when 'the resurrection was the storm centre to an extent it had not been previously and has not been since',[4] all went to great lengths to extol the flesh and its dignity as divine creation, because they were arguing on a background of a widespread repudiation of the physical as having anything to do with God or the spiritual realm. The case with us is rather different. We do not inherit a conviction that there are two spheres, the physical and the spiritual, which are incompatible, and that religion belongs to the latter only. It is rather that in our so-called materialism it has become very difficult for us to think of things and persons except as things-in-themselves and persons-in-themselves, and this aspect of things and persons tends to fill the whole view. It is not simply that the concept of a transcendent God has disappeared or is disappearing, but, and possibly more seriously, that the transcendent quality of things and persons disappears. By transcendent quality here could be meant the quality of possession and non-possession at the same time, the quality of being but of being in conditions which cannot encompass or express or give an explanation of that being without remainder. This difficulty could make itself felt as a difficulty in giving to things and persons a sacramental quality, or as a sense that in attempting to do so one was forcing something alien and extra upon them, rather than bringing to light their true nature, of which they already exhibit certain characteristic signs.

Christian doctrine is not a collection of disjunct items which somehow can be made to add up to a whole, but always a nexus of interdependent truths. To proclaim resurrection except on the basis of creation would be to make of it at best a pious tenet, perhaps related to an isolated fact about man, that he is mortal. But to believe in 'the resurrection of the body and the life everlasting' is only another way of believing in the almighty Father, creator of heaven and earth. For the Christian doctrine of creation has it that the transcendent God has put his hand to the autonomous existence of beings other than himself, for which he is responsible, as he is also responsible for the conditions in which, and the potentialities with which, they exist; and this doctrine itself is not yet fully stated unless and until he is also responsible for the consummation and perfection of what is, even apart from sin, unfinished, but which also has the potentialities for being finished. Creation, and resurrection as the further creative act or acts which are required for creation to be itself, go together. To put it vulgarly, if we have got as far as to believe in the transcendent God as creator, are we not right to demand that he at least has the integrity of any decent artist or craftsman to complete what he has put his hand to, and to see that it becomes what it has it in itself to become? In Revelation the one who sits on the throne says: 'Behold I make all things new.' In relation to the subject of the previous chapter one would have to consider how far, and in what way, this creational language had any bearing on what the historical Jesus conceived himself to be about and to have put his hand to. Or it might be observed that in the context of resurrection Paul, perhaps borrowing from gnostic thought, was compelled to talk in terms of the earthly Adam and the heavenly Adam. These are creational terms, and so perhaps in some of its aspects is the frankly apocalyptic title 'the Son of man', which the evangelists represent Jesus as applying to his own ministry and destiny.

The subject may then be approached from the other end. Resurrection is an eschatological word; of that there can be no doubt. To some extent modelled on beginnings it must necessarily speak of ends, since the beginnings it reflects are really beginnings and not a finished article, whatever difficulties that may bring for stating a doctrine of creation. And it speaks of *the end*, since it speaks of time in relation to a transcendent creator who is responsible for time. Before approaching any problems of translation we have to take stock of the fact that there are a whole host of conundrums here which are inherited from the New Testament itself, and even more from the intervening centuries, when the silences of the New Testament were filled in from Jewish and Christian apocalyptic writings. There is no greater conceptual or doctrinal mess than eschatology. An imminent parousia, a being snatched up to meet the Lord in the air when some will be transformed without death and resurrection; no one resurrected until all are; resurrection of the body in such a form that the major theological concern was how the scattered particles were to be assembled, to which the regular answer was that with God all things are possible; a thousand years reign of the messiah; Armageddon and all that; third, fifth and seventh heavens; thrones, principalities and powers; all that has been dubbed the furniture of heaven and the temperature of hell. One may suspect that all, or almost all, of this is theological junk. It can be eliminated at one stroke by Paul's own quotation, as some think from an apocalyptic work. 'Eye has not seen, nor ear heard neither has entered into the heart of man what God has prepared for those who love him'. None of this is to be translated except after very careful scrutiny indeed, but is rather to be taken as a warning of the complexity and limits of the subject. When it is said, as by Neville Clark in his book *Interpreting the Resurrection*, not with reference to New Testament but to present day belief, that 'the un-veiling of the Resurrection awaits the parousia',[5] does the statement speak to our condition, and, if not, is this because we are simply unconverted or unilluminated at this point? The parousia doctrine is surely irrecoverable in anything like its New Testament form, and was already being dissolved within the New Testament itself to make room for other eschatologies (e.g. those of Ephesians or the Fourth Gospel), and this dissolution may have been the occasion of some of its profoundest insights. The Jewish conception that this present time is to be succeeded by more time or end time was replaced in subsequent centuries, and here and there within the New Testament itself, by the Greek contrast between time and eternity. Is this something simply to be reversed in obedience to a demand for a return to a more 'biblical' doctrine? Is the conception which went along with an expectation of an imminent parousia that resurrection is an inescapably corporate process any longer thinkable, and does it have to be translated? What does the resurrection of the body, which has so vexed Christian thought, say which has to be said, if anything?

But these inheritances from the past, which are due to the break-up of the original complex of thought within which resurrection was contained, and to the speculations which came in to fill the gaps, are not now the real problems for us in our understanding of space and time. The real problem is the evolutionary mode of thinking which has now become our second nature. While materialism might be put at the door of sin and simply condemned with a view to conversion to a better and more realistic view of things, this cannot be said of the revolutionary picture of the created order, which we have inherited recently, and which has become embedded in our thinking about everything. From this, though it may provide us with no particular joy, we see no particular reason to be converted. So long as mankind was thought of as a separate species, created specially and relatively recently for a limited space and time, words like 'creation', 'resurrection' and 'eternal life' could make immediate sense. When, however, the picture in the mind is of man as a species which has developed over aeons of time from an animal past, and which contemplates aeons of time to come, it becomes very difficult to superimpose upon it a different picture conjured up by such words. The popularity of the work of Teilhard de Chardin comes from his attempt to do this, whether legitimately or illegitimately. It may be objected that too much importance is here being attached to the imagination, that doctrinal truth is not imagination, but both controls and outstrips it. Nevertheless, imagination originally played a considerable part in furnishing the thought forms and language of doctrine, which becomes ineffective if it is too far divorced from the pictures in the mind by which men live. The evolutionary process as such provides little by which to extrapolate a significant future, other than that the emergence of man is qualitatively and not simply quantitatively different, in that man is now an animal which knows that it has evolved and that, knowing this, he must now accept responsibility for the control of his future as a race. But this begs the questions of man's nature and goal. Indeed, there is no goal as such, but only the emergence of one generation from the efforts of the preceding. This is as far as the evolutionary mind can go. It may be that in the face of this the emphasis in Christian eschatological language may have to change. In the New Testament the salvation and wholeness of the individual, of which resurrection is a symbol, was bound up with and inseparable from the salvation of the whole, and was imaginatively thought of in this way. This was possible so long as the elect contemplated were small in number and the time short, and it was valiantly kept going down the centuries against increasing odds. But it loses its cogency before the vast spaces and aeons, and in face of the revolution in the mind and imagination the salvation or wholeness of the individual as a microcosm may have to take precedence, and we may have to be largely agnostic about the relation of this to the whole.

In between the beginning and the end is the present time, and one of the most significant developments within the New Testament is the way in which, as a result of the impact of Christ, the thought of resurrection is drawn into the present to bind present and future together before God. What would appear to have happened is that the gospel broke open the fixed schema of Jewish thought, separated out the various elements – death, resurrection, judgment, the Spirit, the elect, eternal life – and permitted each to develop more on its own and to produce its own effects. This may be seen particularly in Paul. He can at times speak formally, as if to a schema, as he does when addressing himself to the problem of the Christians who have died before the parousia (I Thessalonians 4), or of the salvation of Jews and Gentiles (Romans 9-11), or to some extent of the resurrection existence (I Corinthians 15). But he can also speak in a different manner when he appeals to present Christian experience, and especially the Spirit, as the basis of the truth of what he is saying. As is evident especially from Romans, Galatians and II Corinthians, the Christian life for Paul is life in the Spirit, that is, in the effective power and presence of God. This life in the Spirit has at least three special characteristics. These are (i) newness – 'to serve in the newness of the Spirit and not in the oldness of the letter (law)' – and something of what this means is spelt out in Romans 8; (ii) life – the Spirit imparts life and makes alive in contrast both to the law which spells death and to the flesh or unredeemed man, who has the mind of death; and the content of this life is righteousness in contrast to the law's bringing unrighteousness to light and the flesh's absence of righteousness; (iii) it is the first instalment or first fruits, not of more Spirit, but of glory, an eschatological term, which is the nearest the Bible comes to describing the divine nature or life itself. Since for Paul the resurrection also spells newness, life in righteousness and the promise of glory, it is brought into close connection with the Spirit and *vice versa*. It is here that the moral content of resurrection, which was attached to it, though somewhat loosely, through its association with death and judgment, is brought to the front. So it can be said of Christ himself that he 'was handed over for our sins and raised for our justification', or that 'he was designated Son of God with effective power as a result of resurrection and a spirit of holiness'. And it can be said of the Christian that he dies with Christ to sin and rises with him (or will rise with him) to righteousness, or that his justification is unto life. Here resurrection is unhooked from its connection with parousia and becomes creative in the present.

This is the result of the impact of the gospel. In relation to the Jesus of history it would have to be asked how far, and in what way, this impact was a continuation of, or made possible by, what Jesus himself did or said. This would not be in terms of resurrection itself, of which Jesus says almost nothing, and which was certainly not central to his ministry. Again this may be presented through two opposing positions. Ulrich Wilckens maintains the position that the primary meaning of the resurrection of Jesus himself was the ratification of his work by God.[6] There would seem to be a good deal in the New Testament to support this view, and this is how it has generally been understood. Marxsen,[7] however, objects that this is to fit Jesus into a resurrection schema, so that the historical Jesus would be, as it were, merely the precursor of the risen One, and all that he preached and did would stand in a parenthesis, which was removed only by resurrection. His objection is based on the form-critical ground that the units of tradition in the gospels did not convey this in themselves, but only when it was imparted to them as they were made constituents of a single story which moved towards a climax of death followed by resurrection. Once this secondary motif is removed the units speak only of Jesus' direct claim to sovereignty, and of a ministry which itself made an ultimate demand. The only view Marxsen considers deserving of consideration is that what was fundamental was not Jesus' resurrection, but Jesus himself, who in word and action anticipated the judgment and the end, and who faced men with God and brought him near. Through his appearance – whatever that may mean; it was understood at the time as resurrection – this ministry and message were renewed in and through the church. If this is correct, what prepared for the impact of Christ after the resurrection was primarily his affirmation of the kingdom of God, and such continuation as there may have been lies here. But this would be to say that through his previous affirmations the resurrection gospel, when it did appear, had a rootedly moral content. It was concerned in the end with effective life in a world which was God's creation, and this was a life of radical moral obedience. What resurrection says in respect of this is that such a life is itself the gift of God and has its source in him. In saying this it reinforces the doctrine of creation, which also affirms the life of the world to be a given thing, and to be given from a transcendent source. Both the gospel proclamation of the kingdom of God and Paul's proclamation of the resurrection interpret human life in radically moral terms, and the question for human beings is thus whether there are any morally new beginnings, or whether life must always proceed from where it happens to be, with such improvements as the wit of man is able to devise. Though the context in which Paul was led to pose the question – his conflict with the Judaizers – may be completely dated, and his language about justification by works or faith have little if anything to say to us now, the issues he raised may be said to remain, once men are convinced that life in this world is a moral affair. The issue then is whether there is a moral power available which is capable of establishing really new beginnings, and which is thereby capable also of establishing life as being from God. What Paul speaks of in the language of resurrection the Fourth Gospel and the First Epistle of Peter speak of in the language of rebirth or birth from above, which the first connects with eternal life and the second with resurrection. Paul's question, whether a man can be justified by the moral law without setting himself over against God as the giver of his life, appears in the Fourth Gospel in the question of Nicodemus 'Can a man be born again (or, from above) when he is old?' Both answer that there is such a power, which is moral, and which brings with it the recognition that life is from God and to God. This 'from God' and 'to God' are seen as permanently stamped on human life by resurrection. Here there would seem to be a minimum of translating to be done, as the New Testament has itself gone a long way in the process.

Resurrection in the New Testament and Now 77

NOTES

1. *Resurrection and the New Testament* (Studies in Biblical Theology, Second Series 12), SCM Press 1970.

2. W. Marxsen, 'The Resurrection of Jesus as a Historical and Theological Problem', in C. F. D. Moule (ed.), *The Significance of the Message of the Resurrection for Faith in Jesus Christ* (Studies in Biblical Theology, Second Series 8), 1968, pp.32ff., 40ff.

3. W. Pannenberg, *Jesus – God and Man*, Eng. trans., SCM Press 1968, pp.82ff., and 'The Revelation of God in Jesus of Nazareth' in J. M. Robinson and J. B. Cobb (eds.), *Theology as History,* Harper and Row 1967, pp.101ff.

4. See W. C. van Unnik, 'The Newly Discovered "Epistle to Rheginos" on the Resurrection', *Journal of Ecclesiastical History* 15, 1954, pp.143f., 153ff.

5. Neville Clark, *Interpreting the Resurrection*, SCM Press 1967, p.113.

6. U. Wilckens, 'The Tradition-history of the Resurrection of Jesus', in C. F. D. Moule, *op. cit.*, pp.64ff.

7. Marxsen, *art. cit.*, pp.45ff.

6

Is the New Testament Church
a Model?

The question is pertinent in view of the demand for change in the church, if that is not to be a pursuit of change for change's sake, but rather of reformation according to the principle of *ecclesia semper reformanda*. It is also pertinent in view of the ecumenical movement, which is bound to pursue both reunion and reformation at the same time. But both parts of the question constitute a problem. Can one speak of the New Testament church, and in what sense would one wish to use here the word model?

Can one speak of the New Testament church? The problem here is of the same kind as the problem of the quest of the historical Jesus; indeed in some of its aspects it is the same problem from another angle. As Gerald Downing remarks in his book *The Church and Jesus*, which is largely concerned to examine, and report on, the new quest of the historical Jesus, there is also a quest of the primitive church, and he devotes his first two chapters to this. He quotes from John Knox, who is fairly sceptical (though, like Bultmann, not as sceptical as he has been made out to be) about the possibility of discovering the historical Jesus, and who places great weight on the function of memory in tradition, and on the church as the place where Christ is significantly remembered. Knox writes:

It belongs to our existence as Christians to affirm the actuality of Jesus' existence – and not merely the bare facts of it, but something of the full distinctive quality of it. How can this be true in view of the existential certainty of faith, on the one hand, and the tentativeness of all historical findings, on the other? This is the dilemma into which we appear to be inexorably driven. The solution of this problem – or, at any rate, an approach to a solution – lies, it seems to me, in our recognizing, and accepting fully and without reservations of any kind, the radical significance of the early Church. For many of us the problem first came to exist when we saw for the first time that it is the Church, rather than events lying behind it, with which the New Testament puts us directly in touch.[1]

That is, the same critical analysis which creates the problem about the historical Jesus by showing the tradition of his words and acts to have been profoundly affected by the post-Easter faith, also makes one acutely aware of the church. But when the same critical analysis – and by this is meant simply the separation out of the separate strands so that they can speak more for themselves and not only as parts of a harmony – is applied to the evidence for the church itself, can we be as sure as this that we are put into direct touch with something which can be called the 'New Testament church'?

For, in the first place, it would seem to be one of the results of critical analysis of a book as diverse as the New Testament that it puts a question mark against the assumption that there is *a* or *the* New Testament view of anything. It was the aim of biblical theology to show that there was such, and to stress in the variety the unity which is proper to an authoritative holy book. But it would seem to have overstretched itself in the process and to have been responsible for a certain amount of theological whimsy; it is now somewhat in decline before a more rigorous examination of the diversities. This could be of present importance, inasmuch as the ecumenical movement, which would be likely to be concerned with the question how far the New Testament church is a model, has for historical reasons been wedded to biblical theology – is not the Bible the one thing Christians have in common? – and its latest body of recruits, the Roman Catholic Church, has in its recent discovery of biblical studies also tended to be wedded to it.

Secondly, when the critical knife is inserted here a number of questions can be raised, and legitimately raised. It is thus a genuine and not a fanciful question whether Jesus (and we are here back at the quest of the historical Jesus) intended, at any rate in his earthly existence, a church, or anything to which we would now naturally attach the word 'church'. That his mission was to Israel, and that within it he created a community, are probable, perhaps certain. If he created the body of the Twelve, it had meaning in relation to that mission. But the only saying we have about them (in variant form and context in Matthew and Luke) is that they will sit on thrones judging the tribes of Israel. That is, they symbolize the end-point in a time now imminent of the mission of Jesus in judgment and new creation towards Israel. This, perhaps, represented his total horizon on the matter. It is, in any case, one which cannot be shared any longer, and is different from the view of the Twelve as the fountain-heads of apostolic tradition, which they became in the second century, and are on their way to becoming in the New Testament itself. So, said Loisy, 'Jesus foretold the kingdom, and it was the Church that came.'[2] This could be taken to be a cynical statement, but it was not necessarily intended so; and for a theologian to use it so would be to cease to be a theologian and to become a sentimentalist, which is something a theologian must never be. The first fruits of historical criticism may be disillusionment; but disillusionment may be theologically fruitful. That Jesus preached the kingdom of God but the church was the result could direct attention to two truths of permanent importance in the matter. The first is that given currency by John Robinson in the form 'Have as high a doctrine of the Church as you like, as long as your doctrine of the Kingdom is higher',[3] and the second is that there is no doctrine of Christ without a doctrine of the church, no christology without ecclesiology, and *vice versa*. This can be seen semantically. The two earliest and most permanent christological terms are Messiah and Lord, and neither can exist without a correlative. The correlative of Messiah is Israel; the Messiah is Israel's Messiah or God's Messiah for Israel, and there is no Messiah without his elect. The correlative of Lord is slave or slaves, and 'the Lord' seems to have begun life as 'our Lord', and there is no Lord without the community over which he is lord. That is to say, in relation to the subjects of the previous two chapters, that the existence and nature of the church were somehow related to the actions and words of the Jesus of history, though what that relation was is by no means clear. It cannot be simply a relation of continuity or reproduction, since the kingdom of God which appears to be central for the historical

Jesus becomes peripheral in such utterances of the New Testament church as we possess, and messiahship and lordship, which are peripheral in the gospels, have become central for them. And it is to say, secondly, that since christology and ecclesiology are so closely connected, and since christology arises on the basis of belief in the resurrection, ecclesiology is bound to be varied because the tradition about the resurrection exhibits a great degree of diversity and fragmentation. And since resurrection is an eschatological concept, the varied understandings of the church may reflect the varied understandings of eschatology, which some would see as the first theological question which Christians had to face, and the facing of it as the principal cause of theological development.

A rigorous analysis of the New Testament writings does bring to light, alongside the unities they possess, a considerable variety. In some cases it is not easy to say much at all. What kind of church Mark's Gospel was written from or for, and what conception of the church it envisages, are open questions. Is Trocmé correct when in his interrogation of this gospel as to what its author approved of and what he disapproved of he reaches the conclusion that its particular form and tone are best explained as a protest against a falling off in the mission to the Gentiles and the growing power of the James party at Jerusalem which would make Christianity a reformed Judaism perhaps under a caliphate of the family of Jesus?[4] The matter is somewhat clearer in the case of Matthew's Gospel. This is the only gospel which places the word 'church' on the lips of Jesus, once in the famous passage where it refers to 'my', the Messiah's, church built on the rock of Peter, and the other where it means the local community, which exercises discipline over the incorrigible sinner, and where disciples exercise the binding and loosing authority of rabbis. This gospel was early called the ecclesiastical gospel because it most fitted what the church of the second and subsequent centuries had come to think a gospel ought to be and to provide. But it contains puzzling features. It both contains the most explicit statement of the limitation of the mission of Jesus and his apostles during his lifetime to Israel, and also at the point of resurrection breaks these bonds and becomes the most explicitly universal. The church is for all the world, as the Lord is the one who in this gospel alone proclaims himself the universal Lord of heaven and earth; but this Lord is also the universal rabbi, and the function of the church is to make pupils, and to instruct them in Jesus' words, which words in their Matthaean form show ample evidence of modification in the direction of a Jewish-Christian catechesis developed in a church which has lived cheek by jowl with Judaism, and has debated with it what the true Judaism is and to whom the Old Testament rightly belongs.

In the case of John's Gospel the matter is somewhat clearer in one respect, in that we possess, as we do not possess in the case of the other gospels, epistles emanating from the same author or the same milieu, so that gospel and church for which or from which the gospel is written are brought closer together. Nevertheless, these epistles are elusive documents. Though I John appears to be written to Christians over a considerable area by one who stands in a position of authority towards them, and II John and III John furnish us with miniature and fleeting glimpses of one community of such Christians and of a crisis over missionary practice somewhere, they do not enable us to plot the communities geographically, nor to date them exactly, nor to get them into sharp focus. The view of Käsemann[5] deserves careful consideration when he concludes that the ecclesiological accents to be heard in these epistles, and in the Fourth Gospel, and especially in chapters 13-16 of that gospel, where the Lord addresses his own, and in chapter 17 where he prays to the Father for them, are not the accents of what was to develop into the great church, the *una sancta catholica et apostolica*, but those of the sect or conventicle, the intense thought and speech of a closely-knit body of like-minded individuals which is highly conscious of itself as distinct from the surrounding world and the surrounding church, and in which the great doctrine that God is love goes along with a love which is confined to the brethren only. This may explain some of the similarities which have been detected between the Johannine writings and the writings of the Qumran community. And since this was also a characteristic of gnostic groups, it raises the question from the angle of ecclesiology of where this gospel stood in relation to gnosticism. In spite of its passionate assertion of the flesh of Christ did it take over more of gnostic thought than was later to be recognized?

In turning to Acts and Paul we meet the critical problem head on. Nowhere has harmonization, that is, the combination of one class of document with another and the reading of one in the light of the other, exercised greater effect on the church's understanding of itself. Since Acts is the only document in the New Testament to tell a connected story of the primitive church it is naturally taken as a framework, and into this story Paul is drafted, and perhaps domesticated. For Luke there can be no rogue elephants in the church as it makes its victorious way in the world to recommend itself as of divine origin. But, as has been mentioned earlier, this may be methodologically false from the start, and it may first be necessary to ignore the fact that Luke happens to take Paul as the hero subject of the last quarter of his two-volume work, and to try to understand Paul from his own letters. This is difficult to do, if only because the Paul of Acts is to us a thoroughly intelligible figure while the Paul of the epistles is frequently not. Anyone who sets out to study Paul ought at some time to ask himself whether the apostle was not mad. He will no doubt very quickly come to the answer that he was not because of the force, sobriety and continued relevance of what the apostle wrote. But in the short time left to him, which may have amounted to ten or so years when he was on his own and could pursue his own plans, he seems to have contemplated himself and his helpers as solely responsible for the mission to the world apart from Israel. The position which appears to be advanced in the concluding chapters of the Epistle to the Romans is that the prophetic promise that, when God miraculously redeems Israel at the end of the ages, the Gentiles will miraculously flock to Jerusalem as converts to the worship of Yahweh, had been put in reverse, and the plan of God was now to be seen as a detour through the conversion of the Gentiles by apostolic labour, which will bring Israel in. Paul stands at the point where the work is finished in the East and he turns towards the West. Was this not an apocalyptic dream which, so far from taking as a model, we can scarcely comprehend? It was, however, in this context that Paul arrived at the conception of the church as the body of Christ. This conception was to be further developed within the New Testament in the deutero-Pauline letters and in systematic theology, and has recently had a long run amongst us. It is a remarkable conception on any showing, but it must be observed that its meaning depends as much upon the meaning of the word 'Christ' as upon the meaning of the word 'body'. Thus in Ephesians where, as in Colossians, Christ is, for certain reasons germane to the author, expounded as a cosmic figure who in the heavenly places unites into himself all the powers, the church also has become a cosmic entity, compassing not only Jew and Gentile but heaven and earth, and is the means by which the divine truth is made known to these powers. But this is a development. For the Christ of Paul is the Lord in the universal mission, and the church is his body in pursuing the urgent missionary task under the shadow of the end. That task emerges as a possibility solely through what Christ is. Jew and Gentile can be united to God and to one another because they are justified, are right with God, on the basis of Abrahamic faith, which is at the basis of God's dealings with Israel and with all men. The response of faith to the grace or free gift of God releases the Spirit or effective action of God, which is manifest in all manner of charismata or gifts of the Spirit, and not in any ecclesiastical office; and this not only creates the freedom of the Christian man, who is released from bondage to morality (the law) and to the egocentricity of human nature (the flesh) and the anxieties which go with it, but also, and for the same reason, enables all manner of possibilities of human fellowship, love and service of the brethren, and of interdependent relationships.

There are two further and not unconnected points here. Firstly, what we are able to see in his letters, and especially the Corinthian letters, is acute controversy. Paul's opponents also had their conceptions of the church, but these can now only be deduced from his own statements. The controversy appears to be basically the same even though it is conducted on two fronts. In opposition to the Judaizers it involved the repudiation of any religious or moral institution the possession of which is made the ground of a man's relation with God. In opposition to the 'spiritual', who regarded themselves as already in the kingdom and as raised from the dead, and the Spirit and the sacraments as the assured possessions of the elect, it consisted in placing these things under the lordship of Christ, who possesses them and not they him, and who is known until the end by faith and not sight and under the cross. Thus in Paul's letters we do not have a carefully worked out doctrine of the church as an entity in the world, but a battle for its nature with relation to the task to be done. Secondly, we do not know what happened to the Pauline churches later. We catch glimpses of some of them in I Peter, Revelation, I Clement and Ignatius, and it is not clear from such glimpses how far the distinctively Pauline perceptions won the

day. These were to have a delayed action through the preservation
of his letters in the New Testament canon. Meanwhile his insights
were developed and applied to fresh situations in a diffused Pauline
school to which belong Ephesians (Colossians?), Acts and the
Pastoral Epistles.

Here we encounter various forms of romanticism. This word is
not intended in a pejorative sense, but stands for the imaginative
element in doctrine. Romanticism here may be one necessary pole, if
the church is something which can only be spoken of dialectically as
both divine and human. Thus, as noted above, Ephesians extends the
cosmic status of the church alongside the cosmic status of Christ, yet
Christ is still firmly its Lord, since he is now the head into which as
a body it grows. It spans heaven and earth and is now itself an
object of belief, but it is also now based on a divinely appointed
foundation, the apostles and prophets, with Christ as the corner-
stone. In Acts the matter is displayed historically by an ongoing
narrative, and for us more persuasively than by theological statement, especially through Luke's attractive manner of writing. In the
first twelve chapters before Paul takes over, the period is covered
by a selection of some eighteen incidents, of which it is difficult to
say, at least of some, how far they are intended to be typical and rep-
resentative; or even, as in the case of Pentecost and the Election of
the Seven, what it was that actually took place. But a single,
self-conscious body, 'the church', now advances and spreads from
its centre in Jerusalem and on the basis of the apostles who are the
Twelve. In the Pastoral Epistles the situation is different again.
The author is faced with heresy, possibly of a gnostic character,
which perhaps he does not understand, and with which he does not,
as does Colossians, engage in theological dispute. He meets it by
asserting a fixed deposit of credal and catechetical truth, and by a
pattern of ethics which owes something to surrounding codes; and
the principal need, which dictates the form of these letters, is of a
supply of reliable teachers to guard and communicate the deposit and
to embody the ethic.

We thus meet in the New Testament a great variety of views with
respect to what is called in shorthand 'the church in the New Testament', and learned and detailed examinations of the evidence, such
as most recently E. Schweizer's *Church Order in the New Testament*,[6] bear this out. And it can be shown, at least on occasions, that

this was not because for some not altogether clear historical reason Christianity was from the first a kind of hotch potch, which gathered a remarkable variety of people in a comparatively short time (though this may be one factor – the differences between Galilean disciples, Jerusalem Hellenists, Corinthian middle and lower classes must have been considerable), but because there was a veritable ferment of change and development, as particular communities and their spokesmen reacted to situations and explored the preaching and living of the gospel in these situations. It is the task of the theologian to attempt to detect, where the material allows it, this development, and its connection with those situations and with the developments in christology, eschatology, soteriology and anthropology.

In what sense, then, could or should the church in the New Testament serve as a model? Certain senses are surely ruled out: the appeal for example at the beginning of the Anglican Ordinal, since it is not 'evident to all men diligently reading holy Scripture and Ancient Authors that from the Apostles' time there have been these orders in Christ's church...' So also the biblicism of Calvin, who wished to have in the church an instance of every type of minister mentioned in the New Testament simply because it was in the New Testament. Indeed, it could be argued that because something is in the New Testament it should not be in the contemporary church, if that thing could be shown to be indissolubly linked with other things in the New Testament which in the process of development were very properly to disappear – such as an imminent parousia – or which were too closely connected with Jewish origins, such as sacrifice or circumcision. A model generally tends to be seen in what most naturally offers itself as such by being relatively fixed, stable and describable. This might mean that the church of the Pastoral Epistles qualified better than the church, say in the Pauline Epistles or Mark's Gospel; but this would surely be a dubious conclusion to draw. Käsemann can at least begin by deriving encouragement from, and seeing something of a model in, this very diversity.

No romantic postulate, however enveloped it may be in the cloak of salvation history, can be permitted to weaken the sober observation that the historian is unable to speak of an unbroken unity in New Testament ecclesiology. In that field he becomes aware of our own situation in microcosm – differences, difficulties, contradictions, at best an ancient ecumenical federation without an Ecumenical Council. The tensions between Jewish and Gentile Christian churches, between Paul and the Corinthian enthusiasts, between John and early catholicism, are as great as those of our own day. Onesided emphases, fossilized attitudes, fabrications, and contradictory opposites in doctrine, organization and devotional practice are to be found in the ecclesiology of the New Testament no less than among ourselves. To recognize this is even a great comfort and, so far as ecumenical work today is concerned, a theological gain. For, in so doing, we come to see that our own history is one with that of primitive Christianity. Today, too, God's Spirit hovers over the waters of chaos out of which divine creation is to take shape. So it is right to emphasize yet again at this point that Jesus' proclamation of the dawning of God's kingly rule may have conjured up many ecclesiologies, but it remains strangely transcendent over them all and is by them all at best brokenly reflected and not seldom totally distorted.[7]

Whatever else is to be said, something like this needs to be said. Schweizer states it far less rigorously when at the conclusion of the book mentioned above, which is the most detailed examination of the matter now available, he writes:

That variety, indeed, gave the Church trouble, and it was not spared hard and distressing arguments. However, it did not evade them, but found its unity confirmed by simply taking the brotherhood of the Church seriously enough to come to terms with it and with the question that it raised ... It therefore persistently tried, as far as it was at all possible, to eliminate such differences. ... The New Testament Church sustained these very sharply defined groups in the one Church.[8]

What is not clear in this passage – perhaps it is due simply to the difficulties of expression – is what the 'it' is which is being talked about. If the 'variety gave the Church trouble' what was the church to which this variety gave trouble? Was not the variety itself the church? 'The New Testament Church sustained these very sharply defined groups in the one Church.' Is not this a tautologous statement? What was this one church? Is it something behind the scenes which does the sustaining? Is not the church in the sense employed here nothing to be found in the New Testament itself, but what eventually emerges from the experiences partially documented in the New Testament by a process we can no longer trace in detail, and which involved an accepted creed, a canonical scripture now incapsulating the previous variety, and an inter-communicating episcopate? The question then remains what this incapsulated variety in its now canonized scripture has to say to the contemporary church.

It may say something, and so serve as a model, just by being what it is, and by exhibiting life in Christ as having such pertinacity as to exist in such tensions and variety. For then it draws attention to what is perhaps the chief *raison d'être* of the church, to that which has brought it into being and keeps it in being. For the church should constantly be recurring to the question why it exists at all amongst all the other things which exist. What exists is the world, and all that therein is, especially mankind. Whatever is produced by way of corporate living and arrangements must justify itself on the ground that it answers some proper need which is deemed to arise from living in the conditions and circumstances of the physical world, as for example, the state, the educational system, the judiciary, the theatre, sport etc. What need does the church exist to fulfil? Apparently none. It has no *raison d'être* according to the general account of things, but only when the questions are raised whether human existence is a unity, whether what exists is properly called a universe, and whether it is according to the true nature of things to speak of 'mankind' when what we see is a great variety of contrasted and often warring groups. The church can come into existence alongside whatever else exists only in so far as there is already in the human mind by divine creation an ineradicable conviction that true human existence is existence in unities. The utterance of Ephesians, 'One Lord, one faith, one baptism, one God and Father of all, who is above all and through all and in you all', is a Christian and particularly ecstatic expression of this. But it is not itself the invention of Christian faith; it belongs already with the human furniture. However deeply buried, it is there to be evoked. Yet it has to be evoked because it is very deeply buried, and the New Testament shows a particularly powerful evocation of it, which is the more powerful because of the great variety of the circumstances, so that it is not possible to say of the New Testament that it is evidence for the emergence of a religious society of like-minded people who were drawn together by a common religious experience which mapped out one area of human life. Some of the circumstances of these tensions and varieties – for example, the distinction between Jew and Gentile – which belonged to a particular way of looking at the world, may now have little to say, except in those areas such as South Africa which live in a pseudo-biblical world. It is the fact of them at the starting point of Christianity which is possibly of permanent significance, and this is why it is harmful to cover them up.

But here everything always remains to be done. The unity of mankind, and its existence in love in the midst of tensions, are always to be, and never are actually realized. They can hardly be held for long in the mind apart from belief in and adhesion to the one God. How could they be, if that is their ultimate source? New Testament ecclesiology is nothing apart from its christology and its eschatology, that is, apart from the lordship of Christ, which means his capacity to renew, recreate and consummate. It is the witness of the New Testament that the lordship of Christ provides the truest basis for the combination of what in the human mind often appear as contradictory and in conflict, that is, on the one hand the freedom of the individual to be himself as a person, and on the other hand the possibility of a real community of the most diverse individuals. It is of this that the various ecclesiologies of the New Testament are attempted expressions, and they are primarily significant for us in this respect. As institutions or institutional structures they may have no significance at all. As such expressions they bring to light and into effect what lies in humanity for it to be, but which remains partly hidden and ineffective apart from the humanity of Christ. There is not much here by way of model, but perhaps a great deal by way of suggestion and direction.

NOTES

1. J. Knox, *The Church and the Reality of Christ*, Collins 1963, pp.21ff., cited by G. Downing, *The Church and Jesus*, 1968, p.22.

2. A. Loisy, *The Gospel and the Church*, Eng. trans., 2nd ed., Pitman 1908, p.166.

3. J. A. T. Robinson, 'Not Radical Enough?', *Christian Freedom in a Permissive Society*, SCM Press 1970, p.237.

4. E. Trocmé, *La formation de l'Évangile selon Marc*, 1963, chs. II and III.

5. E. Käsemann, *The Testament of Jesus,* Eng. trans., SCM Press 1966, esp. pp.32f., 65ff.

6. E. Schweizer, *Church Order in the New Testament* (Studies in Biblical Theology 32), SCM Press 1961.

7. E. Käsemann, 'Unity and Multiplicity in the New Testament Doctrine of the Church', *New Testament Questions of Today*, 1969, pp.256f.

8. Schweizer, op. cit., §20f (p.169).

7

Commitment

The college of which I have the honour to be a member has two
features in its programme which may be unique. The first is that on
Mondays in the first two terms in the year no one is allowed to
lecture to students (other than students of theology) on their ordinary
subjects between ten o'clock and eleven, in order to leave them free
if they choose – and generally between three and four hundred do so
choose – to attend a course of lectures in theology. The course rotates
in a three-year cycle, and covers biblical, doctrinal and philosophical
theology (or the study of religions). At the end of each year those
who choose may sit an examination on the year's course, and if
successful in all three years are granted an Associateship of King's
College. So, scattered over the globe is a considerable number of
doctors, teachers, scientists, lawyers, engineers, executives and
housewives who not only are entitled to put A.K.C. after their
names, but have submitted themselves to some account of the Christian theological tradition, and have perhaps reflected on what it had
to say with reference to the particular academic discipline they were
studying.

The second feature is that on Fridays in the first two terms in the
year no one is allowed to lecture to the students of theology, of whom
there are generally some two hundred, on their subject between ten
o'clock and eleven, in order to leave them free if they choose to
attend a course of lectures on a subject which is not immediately
theological. The course is devised with great care and skill, and the
subjects treated by experts in the field. I recall two such courses in
particular. The first was headed 'What manner of Man?', and

began with the Professor of Medicine talking on 'Genesis' (by which was meant not the first book of the Bible but human birth, illustrated with slides), and he was followed by experts talking under the titles Chromosomes and Genes; Chemistry, Character and Conduct; The Brain; The Developing Child; Man as a Social Being (the lecturer of course from the London School of Economics across the way); The Mature Man (a Jungian psychologist) and Man and God. One of the reasons I recall the course is that I had to attend it throughout, since I had ('pity me, O my friends') to bring it to an end with Man and God. This was significant of the position of theology. No longer does she preside as the queen of the sciences and lay down at the beginning the direction to be taken. The theologian, if he belongs in this gallery at all, must come at the tail end, and offer such marginal comments as he is able. None of the other lecturers had in any way to justify his existence, for his particular branch of study was accepted as furnishing real information by the particular yardstick he used, and all that was required was that he should continue to improve the yardstick and use it as accurately as possible. So, as the course proceeded, a composite picture of man was built up without ever going outside man's scientific observations about himself. Like that visual aid for children which consists of a cardboard outline skeleton of a man flanked by successive pieces of cardboard on which are traced the bones, the sinews, the nerves etc., and which when folded one over another eventually present a recognizable human being. What manner of man? That is he. Is there any more to be said?

But I recall another of these courses in which, after an introductory lecture by the Professor of English on English Literature since the War, a series of experts from outside the college gave lectures on Sartre, Camus, Brecht, Beckett and so on. All these authors turned out to be either expressed atheists or agnostics yet, as they were expounded, two things appeared to be common to them. They were all intensely theological writers, occupied with ultimate questions even if they never used the word 'God', and their works were marked by a kind of intense agony. This is striking. There would appear to be often more theology on the stage or in the novel than in the pulpit. And man reflecting upon himself finds himself a great problem to himself. The self-consciousness which he possesses, the capacity to reflect on the process of which he is a part, are not apparently of such a kind as to land him into the straight. What then are the character and significance of this capacity for transcending one's environment, of transcending even one's self, and what are its limits? What is this rational mind by which intelligence may reflect even upon itself, and from this reflection may conceive and initiate action? Is it explicable, and in relation to what is it explicable?

From whichever end one starts one seems to converge on the same point. For the theologians theology has tended increasingly to become anthropology. Bultmann is prepared expressly to say so, and to expound Paul in the light of it. Bonhoeffer is, no doubt, a special case from which general deductions should not be made, but he may be in some measure a paradigm of our time in the way in which, as a great churchman, he was first compelled to develop some kind of intense quasi-monastic living for himself and for his students in order to live as a Christian in the world, and was then forced out of it to take the natural, the world as it is, with complete seriousness, to the point in his case of becoming a conspirator. Where do we go if we start from anthropology and its twin, sociology, which are the sciences with which theology will have its chief dealings in the foreseeable future?

The sciences are successful in the use of their several yardsticks in their selected areas of life in that they yield real information. But their success is measured as much by the fact that the information yields power over the environment. Our society is a masterful society because it has increasing mastery over things and can make them do its will. This is immediately inimical to belief in a Creator only if the belief is tied up, as it has often been, with human incapacities, with man's weaknesses and a harping on what he cannot do. But to those who have acquaintance with the Bible this need not be a barrier to belief but rather an aid to it. For according to the Bible the primary commandment of God to man is not a moral commandment in the ordinary understanding of the word, but the command which is coterminous with creation to increase and multiply and subdue the earth. 'This is what it says in the good Book,' remarks the father to his teenage daughter in John Osborne's *Inadmissible Evidence*, 'and by God I believe that your generation has done it.' This is taken up by the psalmist when he says, 'What is man that thou art mindful of him ... thou hast put all things in subjection under his feet.' It constitutes part, perhaps the whole, of what the Old Testament at least means by man being in the image of God. It is not entirely absent from the New Testament gospel of Christ, who is the image of God, and who is depicted as invested with power over heaven and earth, or even perhaps from the somewhat curious and unexplained fact that his ministry was not simply verbal, but was apparently of necessity effected by physical action towards the bodies of men. In so far as we know the mastery of things we begin to know in our bones something of what lordship is. In the only sample of life which we know at first hand, which is ourselves, we know that to be alive feels like being masters of the world, transcending the pattern, discovering the secrets of nature, manipulating it and making it do one's will. The more this happens the more acute becomes the question whether we can ourselves be included in, and absorbed into, the world of which we are a part, and of which we are at the same time the masters through mind. Is the world, of which we can give an increasingly accurate account, an account proved true by the fact that it works, also a world by reference to which alone we can give a satisfactory account of ourselves? Being alive feels like mastery, but it also feels like being mortal, finite, perishable, unable to go on maintaining this mastery always, and having nothing finished or complete, unless we postulate some hypothetical completion for the future of the race which does not seem to be a genuine extrapolation from what being alive feels like in the present. If faith is the appreciation of things as they are, the facts to be appreciated are of this twin kind, that we can account for the world and master it, but cannot account adequately for ourselves in terms of the world we master, and that we can use the world but are unable to assume authority for its existence and authorship.

It is not only mastery, however, that we experience, but a further activity to which we have to give some such word as 'creation', and creation is a different word, and describes a different thing, from the evolution which has gone along with the increasing mastery of the world. In evolution one is studying the principles of generation and emanation. Some things generate or bring into life other things identical with or very like themselves; some things emanate from other things. But in creation there is believed to be an element of the new. Evolution is a redistribution of force and energy, but

creation is more than a redistribution of the old, and involves some
element of the new which is brought about by a certain freedom and
capacity to transcend the present. Creation does not solely master
the environment, but moulds it according to some vision of what it
has it in itself to be. This is not confined to art, in which this free
element is particularly focussed, and one does not have to be a high-
brow to recognize it. Many people come to know it in the family,
for which they would not admit that the word 'reproduction' is
an adequate term. Allied with this creativeness is man's perennial
discontent. Why does he not fit more snugly into his environment?
Is it because he is not capable of giving an adequate account of
himself as a product of the natural world in which he lives, and in
whose processes he participates? He is dependent on his natural
environment, but he makes it human; that is, he introduces a principle of creation into it by a combination of passion, vision, intelligence and reflection. And however much this may be accounted for
as a social product it cannot be wholly so, since it is also a means
by which an individual may stand over against the environment
when that means, as it generally does mean, society. And an omni-
present society is experienced precisely as a threat to man in his
creativity. This is what the fierce protest and agony of much of our
literature is about. But for all its agony, does this literature afford
much clue to this situation? Does it afford a better clue, or even as
good a clue, as the clue that man is this ambivalent being because
creativeness is only possible in a world which has createdness
stamped upon it and is not simply evolving, and because there is a
Creator and not only a process, and that man is a link between an
infinite Creator and a finite world?

The matter may be approached from a different direction in the
following series of quotations from a humanist who feels compelled
to reject a theistic interpretation of human existence as logically
untenable, but also to acknowledge a deeply felt hiatus in experience.

If someone wished to have no truck with half lights and ambi-
valences but wanted to deal only with the clearly rational or the
measurable, one can see his point and sympathize. But if this
cuts him free from religious uncertainty, it also excludes him
from experiences of immense human value ... I am thinking of

wonderment, reverence, love, spiritual openness, and adven-
turousness.[1]

He later proceeds to enquire whether these attitudes could only be
cultivated on an agnostic basis by giving the kind of picture of the
world which could evoke them.

> For many people there are times when the world loses it ordin-
> ariness and takes on a disturbing, derivative, transfigured look;
> when awe deepens to numinous awe. 'Events-in-the-world depend-
> ing upon a source beyond the world' – we are tempted to say that
> this is nonsense and sense at the same time: nonsense to the
> logician, sense to the momentary mystic and poet.[2]
>
> The agnostic lacks an apparatus such as the Christian has in the
> Scriptures, which can guide and control his meditation, and con-
> vert fugitive and rare spontaneous experiences into steady, stable
> attitudes and ways of understanding the world ... We cannot be
> at all confident that 'uninterpreted' religious experiences will be
> as impressive or morally fruitful as experiences taken – even in
> a confused way – as cognitive and as revealing the ultimate nature
> of the world.[3]
>
> The humanist has *too much choice* in the attitude he can
> assume. He may view man's place in the world as a peculiarly,
> awesomely privileged place in the cosmic advance towards more
> and more valuable forms of being; or he can be more keenly
> aware of the coincidence of unplanned events that have made
> him what he is, conscious of himself as a lonely affirmer of values
> in an indifferent world.[4]

The burden of these quotations is the agonizing cleavage between
the deepest human experiences and the world in and through which
the experiences take place, so that the question 'What manner of
man?' can have no satisfactory answer because those experiences
cannot be taken as genuine indications of the nature of the world
we live in. Can this cleavage be overcome?

It is characteristic of man that he is not only the bearer of mind
and transcends his environment and even himself by reflection, but
that he must act, and behind his act is decision. By this he makes
history, which is significant action. But how is he to decide and
with reference to what is he to act? This aspect has been brought to

the front by the existentialist philosophies of our time and by their literature, often cast in dramatic or novel form. Existentialism was born within Christianity itself in Kierkegaard, where it was a way of insisting that nothing was true unless it was true for the inner conviction of the individual and was a truth upon which a man staked his existence, and it was used as a weapon against objectivized and desiccated orthodoxy. Divorced from its Christian context, however, it has been used as if it could do the whole of what needs to be done. Life is what you make it. There is no other structure to it than what you decide in making your decision, for what you decide in such a way as to throw yourself in after it is the ultimate. There is an extreme of subjectivism here in which there is no necessary, or even possible, contact between one person and another. A man's decisions are private to himself. There are no indications and reliable guides in the pattern of the world, and a man's decisions are his affirmation of meaning for himself in a world which in some existentialist writing is simply said to be absurd. Here the cleavage, so far from being overcome, is accentuated, and the division becomes even wider between man the decider, the maker of his own history, and the world in which he makes it.

But the place of decision in human life is a sign that, in order to live worthwhile lives in which they act with freedom and creatively, men must commit themselves. This is something other than the acceptance of that lady whose remark 'I accept the universe' received from Carlyle the rejoinder, 'Gad, she'd better.' To accept could be to remain in one's self-awareness an observer of objects and a spectator of their behaviour. But this is not living. For other people are not simply objects of our observation, as we ourselves know when we refuse to regard ourselves as simply the objects of theirs. It is a mark of the religious attitude that it passes from acceptance of things to commitment to the world, to the embracing of life and the loving of it. Indeed, it has been offered as one definition of religion that it is a total commitment to the whole universe. This formulation immediately brings to light two possibilities which stand on either side, viz. a partial commitment to the whole and a total commitment to the part. Science in all its forms involves a partial commitment to the whole, for to be a scientist a man must be committed and have a sympathy with nature at whatever point he approaches it, but he must also stand away from it. For scientific experiment consists, in Bacon's words, in putting nature to the question, and the scientist can only do that accurately and dispassionately if he also keeps his distance. On the other hand a total commitment to the part constitutes that idolatry with which the Bible is so preoccupied, as when a man is said to be engrossed in his family or to make politics his religion. To say that 'a man makes politics his religion' is immediately recognizable as a misuse of language, since total commitment to a part is idolatry, and true religion is a total commitment to the whole. But then the question is, 'What is this whole, and how is it of such a kind as to call out a total commitment from such a being as man is?' What could possibly merit such commitment? If we are to commit ourselves, a story must be told about us and about the world which both deserves to evoke this commitment and which is believed to be true. And what story is that? If we describe ourselves only in scientific terms, then other men are not proper objects of our total commitment, nor even of our moral duty. For a story to be told which will justifiably evoke our total commitment to the whole it has to be a story about the whole of all of us and about the whole to which we are to commit ourselves. To what should man, who is capable of self-transcendence, commit himself? Can a purely finite value placed upon another carry the weight of commitment to him? Can anyone but the infinite Creator exhaust man's thought and desire without remainder?

One reason for the cleavage we have referred to is the absence of a living and convincing natural theology, and the trouble is that the thing itself has been so thoroughly discredited, and the terms to describe it rendered virtually unusable. Fundamentally natural theology should be a treatment of those aspects of human life which in their parable-like quality exercise a certain compulsion on the mind to direct it towards an apprehension of life's transcendent ground and source. It ought for this reason to remain as close as may be to the common man, since it is his basic experiences which it interrogates. But in its traditional scholastic forms it was rarefied and far removed from the common man, and it brought about its own downfall by attempting too much. From inadequate data about the empirical world it sought to elaborate a tight chain of argument which would furnish a logically conclusive proof. In this form it was incapable of accommodating the vast increase of observed facts, and the logic turned out to be faulty. Nevertheless, the necessity for it in some form remains, because the parabolic quality of life persists. As Professor J. J. C. Smart has observed at the conclusion of a disproof of the validity of the cosmological argument, one still feels one wants to go on asking the questions to which the proof was thought to be an answer.[5] When, therefore, Barthians and others rejected it with horror, and turned impatiently away to construct systems solely within the terms of the biblical revelation, they did theology a grave disservice, and despite its occasional impressiveness and profundity their work may well prove to have been still-born.

If the raw material of a natural theology is the basic experiences of the common man it is with sociology that it will have chiefly to deal, since it is sociology which takes up the findings of the other sciences into itself, and aims to give the most complete account of the patterns of human behaviour. Only it is rare so far to find a professional sociologist who considers in depth the implications of his discipline for religion. A notable exception is Peter Berger in his book *A Rumour of Angels*. He is in no doubt about the threat of sociology to religion. It is, he says, a dismal science from the religious point of view, because it carries still further the relativizing process which the other sciences have begun. Whereas the physical sciences challenge certain accompaniments of the faith and not its heart, the human sciences, history and psychology, penetrated deeper, the first by underlining the historical, i.e. the human elements, in the sacred tradition, and the latter by treating religion as an unconscious projection. But sociology, which succeeds to them, 'raises the vertigo of relativity to its most furious pitch, posing a challenge to theological thought with unprecedented sharpness'.[6] It does this firstly by showing with precision to the religious person the extent to which he has a minority status in society, and thinks less and less like the people around him, or even as he himself thinks in so far as he shares the life around him. Secondly, it offers an explanation of how people or groups come to hold the beliefs they do. A belief is held because it has a 'plausibility structure'. It makes sense, but only so long as one lives in, and is surrounded by, members of the group for which it makes sense. The sociologist provides an account of how the group builds itself up. 'The mystery of faith now becomes scientifically graspable, practically repeatable, and generally applicable.'[7] On the other hand, sociology has it in itself also to relativize the previous relativizers, and so to prevent a surrender to modern viewpoints as though they were some form of absolute immune from analysis to which all else must be referred.

In this situation and from this sociological perspective Berger reaffirms over against the Barthian the liberal starting point in anthropology, with its 'anchorage in fundamental human experience', and suggests that the theological enterprise, at any rate in its beginnings, should be a search for 'signals of transcendence'. By these he means 'phenomena to be found within the domain of our "natural" reality but that appear to point beyond that reality', not in a strict philosophical sense as hitherto, but as 'prototypal human gestures'. His first instance may be cited *in extenso*; it is concerned with the propensity for order, which in the past was the starting point for either the cosmological or the teleological arguments in their scholastic forms.

A child wakes up in the night, perhaps from a bad dream, and finds himself surrounded by darkness, beset by nameless threats. At such a moment the contours of trusted reality are blurred or invisible, and in the terror of incipient chaos the child cries out for his mother. It is hardly an exaggeration to say that, at this moment, the mother is being invoked as a high priestess of protective order. It is she (and, in many cases, she alone) who has the power to banish chaos and to restore the benign shape of the world. And, of course, any good mother will do just that. She will take the child and cradle him in the timeless gesture of the Magna Mater who became our Madonna. She will turn on a lamp, perhaps, which will encircle the scene with a warm glow of reassuring light. She will speak or sing to the child, and the content of this communication will invariably be the same – 'Don't be afraid – everything is in order, everything is all right.' If all goes well, the child will be reassured, his trust in reality recovered, and in this trust he will return to sleep.

All this, of course, belongs to the most routine experiences of life and does not depend upon any religious preconceptions. Yet this common scene raises a far from ordinary question, which immediately introduces a religious dimension: *Is the mother lying to the child?* The answer, in the most profound sense, can be 'no' only if there is some truth in the religious interpretation of human existence. Conversely, if the 'natural' is the only reality there is, the mother is lying to the child – lying out of love, to be sure, and obviously *not* lying to the extent that her reassurance is grounded in the fact of this love – but in the final analysis lying all the same. Why? *Because the reassurance, transcending the immediately present two individuals and their situation, implies a permanent statement about reality as such.*

The parent, Berger contends, must inevitably adopt the role of world-protector, in which is involved not only the order of the particular society to which he or she belongs, but order as such. And since the experience of everything being in order is necessary for the true human development of the child,

> at the very centre of the process of becoming human, at the core of *humanitas*, we find an existence of trust in the order of reality ... If reality is coextensive with the 'natural' reality that our empirical reason can grasp, then the experience *is* an illusion and the role that embodies it *is* a lie. For then it is perfectly obvious that everything is *not* in order, is *not* all right ... The face of reassuring love, bending over our terror, will then be nothing except an image of merciful illusion. In that case the last word about religion is Freud's. Religion is the childish fantasy that our parents run the universe for our benefit, a fantasy from which the mature individual must free himself in order to attain whatever measure of stoic resignation he is capable of.[8]

Another of Berger's 'transcendental signs' is 'play'. Why this may be of particular importance is that the development of modern society is likely to lead to the extension of leisure to hitherto unimagined proportions, and man's outlook on life in general will be considerably influenced by his outlook on this. He will have much more time to play, and much more to play with. Western civilization has in its more recent periods been centred on work, interpreted either as a punishment for sin or as a moral duty. This is theologically closely aligned to the doctrine of justification by works. One's activity must be made plausible to oneself and to others by being seen to be useful, profitable or serviceable, because it purchases the wherewithal to go on living, or because it contributes to the well-being of the community. Work is in need of justification by reference to the something else for which one works. In that case play can only be an interruption of work and itself needs justification on the ground that man is physical and mortal; its purpose is to recharge the cells for more work. In itself it is suspect; one ought not to be caught doing nothing. But play and true leisure properly belong in that category of activity which does not need justification. They belong with art in all its forms, and also with worship – true worship that is, for false worship is false precisely because it is engaged in so as to bring about some result. You may not ask an artist what he is painting, composing or writing for, as there is properly no answer to the question. This is an aspect of existence which can even lend itself to systematic exploration along more traditional and systematic lines, as in J. Pieper's *Leisure: the Basis of Culture*,[9] where Aquinas is shown to have had important insights on it.[10] In treating it in more general terms as an important 'signal of transcendence' Berger refers to Huizinga's analysis of play as an element which is indispensable to any culture and which creates its own universe and its own time. 'In the "serious" world it may be 11 a.m., on such and such a day, month and year. But in the universe in which one is playing it may be the third round, the fourth act, the *allegro* movement, or the second kiss.'[11] And since the intention of play is joy, it points in the midst of time in the direction of eternity, and he quotes the words of Nietzsche's *Zarathustra*: 'All joy wills eternity – wills deep deep eternity.'

The word 'commitment' has emerged amongst so many different groups of people to express their fundamental apprehension of what is involved in human living that some theologians have taken it to be the most significant bridge word between Christian theology and secular thinking. To mean what it says, however, it implies the ability to tell a plausible story about the universe. The beginnings of this story must always be with some sort of natural theology. The question for more specifically Christian theology would then be whether the Christian story is necessary to complete it, and whether it provides the fullest, most reliable and most convincing plausibility structure.

The story would run somewhat as follows – though not all parts of it would be equally necessary. The infinite, omnipotent, all-wise and loving God, by a decision beyond our understanding (but perhaps because he is in his essence love) shares his own existence with

others under finite conditions by bringing into being alongside himself a universe (we would have to have a special word for it,
'creation', because it is unlike anything we are directly aware of,
though there may be hints of it around, e.g. in art), and by seeing to
it that there should emerge from its mud ('dust' would be the biblical word) some who are in his image as being personal. As such they
have it in them to master the environment of which they are themselves a part, and by the same faculty are able to reorder and trans-
mute the casual sequences of nature so as to make history. In this
same capacity of freedom lies also the power to introduce schism into
the world and into their own natures by attributing to themselves
something beyond the lordship of the world, viz. the lordship of
themselves, as though they had authorized themselves, and so either
to reduce their stature from that of temporal beings related to the
eternal to that of temporal only, or to invest themselves, or some
created object or vital force, with an absolute significance it is not
able to carry. The story would go on how this God inserted his
influence more directly into this world (we should have to have a
special word for it, 'revelation', because it is not like anything we
know directly, though poetry and vision may hint at it), through a
family, or rather a person, Abraham, but him considered as the
potential father of a family. This family becomes a nation, though
without ceasing to be a family, since God says of its ruler 'I will be
to him a father and he shall be to me a son',[12] and it learns about
nationality that it is the Most High who rules in the kingdoms of
men. Within this nation-family this God confers upon men supreme
dignity, and reveals to them the fullness of their natures, by uniting
himself to human nature and conditions, and human nature and
conditions to himself by way of a man. This is a man whose words
and actions have a consistent intention of holding human life to its
source beyond itself, and whose life is such that men are able to
apprehend this God as the ground of his being and theirs. Through
this man distortions of human life are brought to a head in crucifixion, and are resolved by resurrection, so that it can be glimpsed
how to the obedient and loving will all things come as grist to the
mill, and may be the raw material for a cleaving to God and to
others which is deathless. There is – so the story continues – released
by God through this man into the world in its full capacity a holy
spirit, which is able to penetrate to the inner springs of human

nature, to induce it to die to its distortions, and to cease to justify itself to itself or by reference to anything else than that it receives its powers from God. And this spirit inserts itself between one person and another to persuade them to regard each other in the same way as God regards each of them. Particularly this spirit operates in and through a society which is historically descended from the nation-family of Abraham, but which is unique in being, as the product of this spirit, one; one despite the fearful fragmentation wreaked upon it by time, because rooted in a common humanity which men do not come by through heredity or environment, but which is conferred on them through the man with whom God has united himself; which is holy, in that it shares his union of the temporal and the eternal, and has as a principle of life that its members confess their unholiness, which is some form of denial of this union, and in so confessing are renewed; which is catholic and apostolic, because possessed of a unifying principle of life of more than evolutionary origin and of a truth which is not purely relative. Through this spirit, men are ever and again able to treat the world of which they are a part as divine creation, neither repining at its incompleteness nor attempting to import into it a false completeness and satisfaction of their own making, but finding in its incompleteness evidence of a createdness and given-ness which directs their attention to the giver, who as such will also be the completer.

This is the kind of story we should have to tell in the hope that men will recognize themselves as belonging somewhere within it, and that it will evoke a total commitment of themselves to the whole. There are some who would say that we should content ourselves simply with telling this story over and over again with the necessary elaborations, and that anything else is at best a waste of time, and possibly blasphemous. I respect them, for some of them are great theologians, but I cannot agree with them, for two reasons. Firstly, in telling this story we have to use language of some kind. Where do we get it from? From human life, of course. The words we use – birth, father, love, family, nation, society, mind, will, intention, spirit etc. – come from human experience, and there is no other source of them. It is true that when they are used in our story they tend to be used in a new way, and may be used to say and do things which they do not ordinarily say and do because they are now used about God and life in relation to God. They thus become symbols. It is significant that all the words in our story are symbols, and significant that the man who stands at the centre of the story spoke almost always indirectly and in parabolic language drawn from a wide variety of natural processes and a wide range of human behaviour. Here we have to part company with some. If the modern philosopher is right when he says, 'Reality is accessible to human knowledge only if it is divided into compartments each marked and labelled in syllabus and library ... for all genuine knowledge is specialized knowledge and cannot be anything else', then we cannot begin. Unless somehow, somewhere, some words from our finite and scientifically compartmented and labelled existence have inserted themselves into the mind as symbols and shadows of a more than finite existence our story cannot start. But then we have to ask whether in the story we are man-handling and distorting the words and the experiences they express, or are carrying further something which has begun to appear already in the analysis of life itself? Are we using fantasy words to tell a fairy tale which has no purchase on the real world, or are the words we use already on the way to becoming symbols?

Secondly, the Christian story is given to us not by our natural existence but by revelation. We would not know it, had not God let us know it. But it is none the less a story about man, and we tell it with confidence not only because we believe that God has let us know it but also because we believe it to be the truth about man. It is true also that in hearing it we learn also for the first time a great deal about man which we did not know before. But not everything about man, for it is not our only source of knowledge about ourselves. And from time to time we have to ask ourselves the question whether we are in actual fact the kind of beings we would have to be if the Christian story about us was true. Supposing we were to come to the conclusion that man is in fact a very different kind of being from that which the Christian story presupposes him to be, then no amount of shouting the story at the top of one's voice will do. Here each man is his own theologian. We do not have an option in this matter between being theologians or not, but only between being good or bad theologians. And the theological question is whether man in his hereditary pattern and environment, in actual fact and behaviour, is the sort of being he would have to be if the Christian story about him were true.

NOTES

1. Ronald Hepburn in *Religion and Humanism* (BBC 1964), pp.17f.
2. *Ibid.*, pp.16f.
3. *Ibid.*, p.86.
4. *Ibid.*, pp.83f.
5. J. J. C. Smart, 'The Existence of God', *Church Quarterly Review* CLVI, 1954/55, pp.178ff.
6. P. Berger, *A Rumour of Angels*, Allen Lane 1970, pp.39f.
7. *Ibid.*, p.47.
8. *Ibid.*, pp.67ff.
9. J. Pieper, *Leisure: the Basis of Culture*, Eng. trans., Faber and Faber 1952.
10. And see now Harvey Cox's stimulating if erratic *The Feast of Fools*, Oxford University Press 1970.
11. Berger, *op. cit.*, p.72.
12. II Sam. 7.14.

INDEX

Index of Subjects

Agnostic, agnosticism, 95f.
Anthropology, 86, 100
Apostle, apostolic, 25ff., 85
Ascension, 11

Baptism, 11, 12
  heretical, 11
  infant, 11
Bible, the, 14, 18, 21, 23, 29, 30, 31, 33, 38, 39, 46, 47, 53, 93, 98
Biblicism, 86
Bishops,
  consecration of, 12
  election of, 11

Canon, the, 9, 10, 23, 24, 29f.
  Muratorian, 8, 16f.
  New Testament, 7, 8
Children, teaching the New Testament to, 37ff.
Christian faith, religion, 2, 15f., 24, 63
  authoritative?, 36
Christology, 80, 81, 86
Church, the, 2, 7, 16, 17, 18, 37, 38, 52, 78ff.
  Hellenistic, 19
  New Testament, 78, 79, 86ff.
  Roman Catholic, 16, 79
Commitment, 91ff.
Creation, 69ff, 94, 95, 103
Creed, the, 9f., 39
Cross, sign of the, 11

Demythologizing, 19, 32, 68
Divino Afflante (papal encyclical), 14

Easter, 11, 12
Election of the Seven, 85

Eschatology, 29, 71, 73, 81, 86, 89
Eucharist, the, 11
Evolution, 94f.
Exegesis, 31, 33
  allegorical, 9, 32
Existentialism, 97

Fasts, 12
Fathers, the, 9ff., 18
  Alexandrian church, 32
Form-criticism, 19, 54

Gnostics, Gnosticism, 32, 58
God language, 69

Heretics, heresy, 10
Hermeneutics, 33, 34, 39
History, 1, 59f., 68
  Jesus of, 51ff., 79f., 80f.
Holy Spirit, 11, 13, 14, 15, 16, 74
Humanism, humanist, 38, 47, 49, 96

Images, veneration of, 12
Interpretation of scripture, 31
  figurative, 31
  methods of, 31, 33
  typological, 31, 33
Islam, 35

Judaism, 51f., 81, 82
Judaizers, 76, 84

Kingdom of God, 12, 45, 46, 60, 62, 75

Law, the, 4, 25, 42, 43

Marxism, 38
Morality, 42f.

New Testament, 2f., 5, 6, 7, 8, 13, 14, 17, 18, 19, 22f., 24, 25, 27, 30, 31, 32, 34, 36, 41, 42, 43, 45, 49, 55, 57, 58, 59, 60, 64ff., 78ff.
resurrection in, 64ff.

Old Testament, 2f., 4, 5, 6, 8, 13, 14, 17, 18, 24, 25, 26, 33, 34, 35, 45, 47, 65

Parables, the, 45f.
Parousia, the, 71f., 74
Pentecost, 11, 12, 85
Physical sciences, 99
Priesthood, 25, 35
Psychology, 99

Qumran scrolls, 65
Qur'an, 23, 35

Reformation, the, 12, 17f.
Religions,
comparative study of, 48
non-Christian, 21f.
Religious experience, 40f.
Resurrection, the, 19, 27f., 59, 61, 64ff., 103
Revelation, 103

Romanticism, 85

Sacrifice, 25, 35
Salvation history, 29, 59
Schools, 39f.
Science, 97f.
Scripture, 1ff., 22f., 30, 32, 49
apostolic, 25
Secularization, 35f.
Shaliach, 28
Sociology, 99f.
Son of man, the, 46
Soteriology, 86
Sunday, keeping of, 11

Theology, 19, 21, 37, 49, 92, 93, 98f., 102
natural, 99, 102
Tradition, 1ff., 21f.
apostolic, 26
Trent, Council of, 10, 11, 12ff.
Typology, 33f.

Vatican II, 14, 16

Word of God, the, 6, 7, 18
Worship, 45

Index of Names

Abbott, W. J., 20
Abraham, 103, 104
Aland, K., viii, x, 16, 20
Ambrose, St, 9
Aquinas, St Thomas, 12, 102
Augustine, St, 11

Bacon, F., 98
Barrett, C. K., 7
Basil, St, 11
Beckett, S., 92
Berger, P., 99, 100, 101, 102, 106
Blackman, E. C., 19
Bleeker, C. J., 36
Bornkamm, G., 51
Bouyer, L., 10, 18, 19
Brandon, S. G. F., 23, 36
Brecht, B., 92
Bruce, F. F., 36
Bultmann, R., 19, 20, 51, 78, 93

Calvin, J., 86
Camus, A., 92
Carlyle, T., 97
Cassian, John, 32
Chesterton, G. K., 1
Cicero, 41
Clark, N., 72, 77
Clement of Alexandria, St, 9, 24
Clement of Rome, St, 5, 8, 19, 26, 36, 84
Cobb, J. B., 77
Coleridge, S. T., 23
Congar, Y., 11, 12, 13, 16, 19
Cox, H., 106
Cullmann, O., 17, 29, 30, 36, 59

Dodd, C. H., 3, 19, 44, 50

Downing, F. G., 52, 63, 78, 89
Dufrenne, M., 19

Ebeling, G., 51
Enoch, 23

Freud, S., 101
Fuchs, E., 51

Galileo, 53
Goldman, R., 40

Haenchen, E., 8
Hanson, R. P. C., 9, 19
Harnack, A. von, 6, 19, 24, 36
Hepburn, R., 106
Herder, J. G., 53, 63
Hippolytus, 8
Homer, 23, 53
Huizinga, J. H., 102

Ignatius, St, 5, 6, 19, 84
Irenaeus, St, 7, 9, 15, 17

James, St, 25
Jeremias, J., 46
John, St, 25, 59, 82
John XXIII (pope), 14
John Damascene, St, 12
Jude, St, 25
Julius Caesar, 42
Justin Martyr, St, 6, 26, 36

Kähler, M., 56, 58, 63
Käsemann, E., 38, 50, 51, 60, 63, 86, 90
Kierkegaard, S., 97
Kittel, G., 27

Knox, J., 78, 89
Knox, W. L., 5, 19

Leo I, St, 12
Lightfoot, R. H., 6
Loisy, A., 80, 89
Luke, St, 12, 25, 26, 27, 28, 41, 42, 46, 54, 57, 83, 85
Luther, M., 31, 36

Marcion, 7, 8
Mark, St, 25, 46, 54, 61, 81, 86
Marxsen, W., 67, 68, 75, 77
Matthew, St, 25, 26, 46, 61, 81
Moeller, B., 31, 32, 36
Moses, 23, 33
Moule, C. F. D., 77

Napoleon, 52
Newman, J. H., 16
Nietzsche, F. W., 102

Origen, 9, 19, 24, 32
Osborne, J., 93

Pannenberg, W., 67, 68, 77
Papias, 6, 17, 25
Pasolini, P. P., 63
Paul, St, 3, 4, 6, 8, 16, 24, 25, 28, 34, 41, 42, 44, 59, 66, 67, 71, 72, 74, 76, 82, 83, 84, 85, 87, 93

Paul VI (pope), 14, 43
Peter, St, 25, 26, 81
Philo, 44
Pieper, J., 102, 106
Plato, 33
Potter, D., 63

Rengstorf, K., 27
Robinson, J. A. T., 80, 90
Robinson, J. M., 77
Rupp, E. G., 36

Sartre, J.-P., 92
Schonfield, H. J., 63
Schweitzer, A., 51, 63
Schweizer, E., 85, 87, 90
Smart, J. J. C., 99, 106
Socrates, 42
Streeter, B. H., 19

Tavard, G. H., 13, 19
Teilhard de Chardin, R. P., 73
Tertullian, 10, 11, 12
Trocmé, E., 61, 63, 81, 90

Unnik, W. van, 77

Virgil, 32

Widengren, G., 6, 35, 36
Wilckens, U., 75, 77

HIEBERT LIBRARY

3 6877 00008 4276

M

BS
2395
E9

Evans, Christopher Francis.
　　Is 'Holy Scripture' Christian? and other questions [by] Christopher Evans.　London, S.C.M. Press, 1971.

　　x, 112 p.　23 cm.　£1.75　　　　　　　　　　　　　B71-17643

　　Includes bibliographical references.

HIEBERT LIBRARY
PACIFIC COLLEGE · M. B. SEMINARY
FRESNO, CALIF. 93702

13256

　　1. Bible. N.T.—Addresses, essays, lectures.　　I. Title.

BS2395.E9　　　　　　　　　225'.08　　　　　　72-879401
ISBN 0-334-00723-2　　　　　　　　　　　　　　　MARC

Library of Congress　　　　　　72